THE SPARTANS

TEXT BY
NICHOLAS SEKUNDA

COLOUR PLATES BY
RICHARD HOOK

OSPREY
MILITARY

First published in Great Britain in 1998 by Osprey Publishing,
Elms Court, Chapel Way, Botley, Oxford OX2 9LP, United Kingdom.
Email: osprey@osprey-publishing.co.uk

Also published as Elite 66 *The Spartans*

ISBN 1 85532 948 4

Editor: Iain MacGregor
Design: Alan Hamp @ Design for Books

Filmset in Singapore by Pica Ltd.
Printed through World Print Ltd., Hong Kong

FOR A CATALOGUE OF ALL BOOKS PUBLISHED BY OSPREY MILITARY,
AUTOMOTIVE AND AVIATION PLEASE WRITE TO:

The Marketing Manager, Osprey Direct USA, PO Box 130,
Sterling Heights, MI 48311-0130, United States of America.
Email: info@OspreyDirectUSA.com

The Marketing Manager, Osprey Direct UK, PO Box 140, Wellingborough,
Northants, NN8 4ZA, United Kingdom.
Email: info@OspreyDirect.co.uk

VISIT OSPREY'S WEBSITE AT:

http://www.osprey-publishing.co.uk

Acknowledgements

I would like to thank my friends Richard Catling and Richard
Brzezinski for their help in writing this book. It would not have been
possible to carry out the research upon which this book is based
without the resources of the Ashmolean Library, and I would also
like to express my thanks to that institution and its staff.

Editor's note

Readers wishing to pursue the references to the ancient sources in
the text, can find the abbreviations used in the *Oxford Classical
Dictionary*. Except where it is clearly stated to the contrary, all dates
referred to in the text are BC.

**This 'heroic' statue, found in
Sparta and once thought to
portray Leonidas, is too early for
Greek portraiture, which only
really became popular from
c.475-450. Any surviving portraits of persons living earlier
than this date are likely to be
supposed likenesses, made at a
later date. Busts once imagined
to portray Leonidas or Pausanias
have now been demonstrated to
portray the poet Pindar. (Sparta
Museum)**

FRONT COVER: Sparta Museum.
BACK COVER: Wadsworth Atheneum, Hartford. Gift of J. Pierpont Morgan.

THE SPARTANS

INTRODUCTION

During a protracted series of campaigns against Thebes in the 370s the allies of Sparta declared that they were no longer willing to serve under Sparta's leadership when the allies had so many soldiers and the Lakedaimonians had so few. The Spartan king Agesilaos commanded the allies and the Lakedaimonians to sit apart. The army herald then commanded the potters to stand up, then the smiths, then the carpenters, the builders and so on through all the crafts. Practically all the allies had stood up, but not one of the Lakedaimonians, because they were forbidden to learn or practise a trade. Then Agesilaos said with a laugh 'You see men, how many more soldiers than you we are sending out!' *(Plut., Vit. Ages. 26).*

In fact the Lakedaimonians were the only full time army in ancient Greece and were thus truly an elite force. The institutions of the state and the system of education were organised with a view to creating superbly trained soldiers. Isocrates *(6. 81)* compared the Lakedaimonian political community to a military camp and Aristotle *(Pol. 2. 6. 22)* criticised the Lakedaimonian constitution because it was organised entirely to promote military virtue. Consequently, he stated, the Lakedaimonians did not know how to live at peace when they had won their empire.

Historical outline

The city of Sparta lies in the valley of the River Eurotas, enclosed by the mountains of Taygetos to the west and Parnon to the east. It was just one of the cities of the ancient Greek state called Lakedaimon. Although Sparta's early history is not clear, by the end of the 8th century most of the other cities of Lakedaimon had been reduced to subject status. Their inhabitants were called *perioikoi*, or 'those dwelling about'. Though these communities remained self-governing, they had no power over foreign affairs, for these were decided by citizens of Sparta – the Spartiates – and although people of the state were officially called 'the Lakedaimonians', only the Spartiates held political office and made state decisions.

The word Lakonia describes the geographic area of Lakedaimon; and the adjectival form Lakonian is used to describe the local dialect, dress and so on of the inhabitants.

Other communities lost their independence and became helots, or slaves, of the Spartiates. The Spartans became a slave society, and the helots produced the tithes

3

which enabled the Spartans to train for war full-time. The spectre of helot revolt, which could threaten the entire existence of the state, loomed constantly.

According to tradition, the Lakedaimonian constitution was founded by one Lycurgus. Over the years all elements in the constitution of the Classical period were attributed to him. It is obvious, however, that the constitution grew incrementally. Lycurgus, if he was not merely a fictional character, was responsible only for an earlier form of the constitution.

Sparta was ruled by two kings, one each from two separate royal families – the Agiads and the Eurypontids. These kings took command of the army in time of war. After the end of the 6th century one of the kings would command the army on campaign, while the other stayed at home. The kings held seats on a council of elders, the *gerousia*. The other 28 members were citizens aged over 60 who had been selected for service for life. The *gerousia* prepared business for a citizen assembly which could only accept or reject legislation. The assembly decided on war and

RIGHT **Lakonian warrior statuette from Ayios Kosmas in Kynouria, a disputed area of land lying between Lakedaimon and Argos.** (National Museum Athens)

BELOW **The Southern Peloponnese in the Classical period.** (Nick Sekunda)

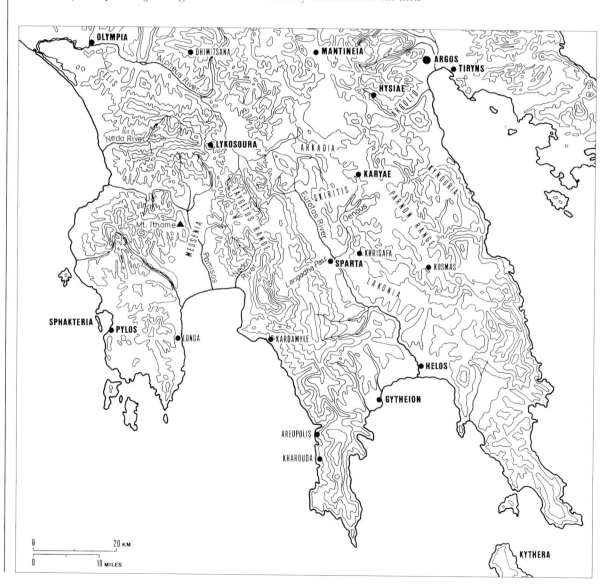

5

peace and ratified treaties; it also had the right to decide on the royal succession, to appoint military commanders and to elect members of the *gerousia* and the five ephors (magistrates). The ephors exercised general control over the kings. They could summon a king to appear before them and could prosecute him through the *gerousia*; they presided over both the *gerousia* and the assembly, and they gave orders for the mobilisation of the army. Two ephors accompanied the king on campaign.

With control of Lakedaimon assured, neighbouring Messenia was conquered during the First Messenian War of 735-715. Most of its land was captured and most of its population became helots. Argos now became the main enemy in a prolonged struggle for dominance in the Peloponnese. A heavy defeat inflicted by the Argives at Hysiai in 669 seems to have provoked a major Messenian uprising – known as the

Grave stele of the Athenian Stratokles, dating to the end of the 5th century. His opponent, wears a pilos-helmet and an *exomis* pinned up at the right shoulder and is carrying a short sword. He may be a Lakedaimonian, though he does not wear the long hair typical of a Lakedaimonian warrior. (Museum of Fine Arts, Boston)

Second Messenian War – which was suppressed with difficulty. The war songs written by the poet Tyrtaios to put heart into the Spartans fighting in this war, became deeply embedded in Spartan military culture.

Expansion continued throughout the early 6th century, this time into southern Arcadia, under the joint rule of the kings Leon and Agasikles. Wars were fought with Orchomenos and Tegea. Eventually the Lakedaimonians changed their policy. In the middle of the century Tegea was brought into alliance, and eventually most of the states of the Peloponnese were brought into a league, with Lakedaimon at the head. Leadership of the 'Peloponnesian League' gave Lakedaimon the legal and moral authority to lead the Greeks during the Persian Wars. The Lakedaimonians, led by the ephor Chilon and the kings Ariston and Anaxandridas, also engaged in military operations to topple tyrannies all over the Greek world, winning even more prestige for the state.

The Greek tyrants were unconstitutional monarchs, often noted for their cruelty and disregard of the law. Anaxandridas' son Cleomenes continued with these practices. Naxos was liberated in 517 and Athens in 510. Cleomenes inflicted a crippling defeat on Argos in 494 at Sepeia which prevented her arch-rival from giving the Persians military support.

Fragment of a 6th century stone statue of a warrior wearing a Corinthian helmet. (Sparta Museum)

Lakedaimon played a key role in the Persian War. However, the regent Pausanias, though victor at Plataea, plotted to bring Greece under Persian domination. Consequently, Lakedaimon lost much of her prestige. The Athenian leader Themistocles also worked against Lakedaimon's influence and built up Athenian imperial power. However, possibly the greatest blow to Lakedaimonian supremacy was the catastrophic earthquake which struck Sparta in 464. A third Messenian War followed (465-460) and then the First Peloponnesian War with Athens (460-446), both of which Lakedaimon survived, though with its manpower severely reduced. In 431 Lakedaimon was dragged into the Peloponnesian War with Athens when its allies threatened to leave the alliance if Lakedaimon could not defend them against Athenian expansion. Lakedaimon survived this war too.

Victory over Athens was achieved by Lysander's co-operation with Persia. Lysander set about building up a Spartan empire in the cities he liberated from the Athenians, setting up 'governments of ten' to replace the democracies and placing Lakedaimonian garrisons and governors (harmosts) in the cities he liberated. Naval victory was achieved in the final phases of the Peloponnesian War, thanks largely to Lysander, who inflicted a crushing defeat on the Athenian fleet at the Battle of Aigospotamoi. Following Lakedaimonian victory in the Peloponnesian War and the empire-building activities of Lysander in the Greek states of the eastern Aegean coast, desultory war broke out with the Persian satrap Tissaphernes in 400.

The Spartan king Agesilaos, who was sent out to Asia in 396, achieved considerable success but was recalled to defend Lakedaimon from a new

Stone statue of a Lakonian warrior or king from Samos. Tensions existed between Samos and Sparta, culminating in a Spartan invasion in the 520s. (Antikensammlung, Staatliche Museen zu Berlin, Preussischer Kulturbesitz)

anti-Lakedaimonian coalition of Greek states. The construction of a Persian fleet made any return to Asia impossible, and the Lakedaimonians were forced to accept a peace which handed Asia back to the Persians. The Lakedaimonians surfaced from the Corinthian War in Greece with a number of imperial commitments but without the military strength to carry them out. Their weakness was fully revealed by their defeat at the hands of the Thebans at Leuctra in 371. Had the Theban general Epaminondas not died at Mantineia in 362, it is doubtful that Lakedaimon would have survived with its territories intact.

ORGANISATION

Training

When a boy was born he was shown to the elders of the tribe, and they decided whether he would be reared or left to die in a gorge on Mount Taÿgetos. At home the young boy was taught to be content with plain food and not to be afraid of the dark or of being left alone. His mother would bathe him in wine to 'temper' his body.

Military training started for the young male Spartan at the age of five when he became a 'boy' (*paidion*), a status which lasted six years. He left home and started to live in barracks. He learnt the *pyrriche*, a dance while carrying weapons which trained the young man in his movements under arms *(Athen., 630-1)*. He would also learn by heart all the songs of Tyrtaios which were sung on campaign. He was enrolled in a 'pack' and encouraged to compete against other packs in sports. He was also taught

to read and write. At the age of ten he would begin to take part in competitive exercises in music, dancing and athletics.

On completion of his 12th year the boy became a 'youth' (*meirakion*). His physical exercise was increased; he had his hair cut short; he went barefoot to toughen his feet for battle; his tunic was taken away; and he wore only one thin cloak in summer and winter alike to prepare him to withstand extremes of heat and cold. For the most part he played naked. He would live in barracks, sleeping alongside the others in his pack on a bed made from reeds plucked by hand from the valley of the River Eurotas. In the winter he was allowed to add thistle-down to his bed, as

11

Small, black-glazed Lakonian pot in the shape of a Corinthian helmet, probably intended to hold perfume and probably dating to c.600-575. Note the pointed moustache. (Sparta Museum).

it was thought this material had some warmth in it. The youth was fed on a minimal diet so he could work on an empty stomach in the future. It was also believed that a diet that made a youth slim would make him grow tall. He was allowed to supplement his diet by stealing, in order to increase his cunning; this would be useful in war. If caught, he was heavily punished – for being caught rather than for stealing!

Each Spartan youth had an adult guardian, called a 'lover', who was responsible for his conduct. According to Xenophon *(Lak. Pol. 2. 13)*, engaged in a work of praise for the Lakedaimonian constitution, such connections were banned if they were formed on a purely physical basis, however he did not expect his reader to believe him. There can be little doubt that pederasty was common, and that a large percentage of the adult male population were practising homosexuals. The state could not tolerate bachelorhood, though, as its military manpower had to be maintained, and if citizens did not marry by a certain age, they were publicly humiliated. Thus we find King Agesilaos happily married yet an ardent admirer of boys. Bisexuality of this type was quite widespread in many ancient Greek states.

When a male had completed his 18th year he became an adult citizen (*eiren*). For his first year he would serve as a trainer of the youths. After that he would enter one of the Spartan messes, which housed about 15 males from various age-classes. The age at which a Spartan adult was allowed to live at home with his wife is not entirely clear, but he was not permitted into the marketplace to converse with his fellow adults until the age of 30.

When not on a military expedition, a Spartan spent his time in choral dances, feasts and festivals, hunting, physical exercise and conversation. As Plutarch puts it *(Vit. Lyc. 22. 2)*, the Spartans were the only men in the world for whom war was a welcome rest from training for war. The Spartan remained liable for military service outside Lakedaimon until 40 ears from his coming of maturity *(Xen., Hell. 5. 4. 13)*, though we hear of one Hippodamas who died in battle in 364 at the age of 80.

Every Spartan was liable to be conscripted into the secret service (*krypteia*) for two years before the age of 30. Upon entering office, the ephors always declared war on the helots in order that there would be no impiety involved in killing them. From time to time (presumably when threatened by revolt), they sent out groups of young men into the countryside equipped with only daggers and rations. They hid out in remote places by day, but by night they stalked the roads and killed any helot they came upon. Sometimes they would kill the strongest helots as they worked in the fields. We know nothing about their activities in more normal times. Perhaps they patrolled against robber gangs, gathered intelligence and maintained security in the countryside.

Hoplite organisation

A great deal of evidence has survived concerning Spartan military organisation, but much of it is contradictory. It is clear that the structure of the army was subject to periodic reorganisations – a view generally held in the 19th century and still held by some today. However, in recent years a different train of thought has emerged, namely that the structure of the army remained substantially unchanged from remote antiquity through to the Classical period. In the opinion of the author, there is as yet no satisfactory position on this.

Surviving fragments of the poems of Tyrtaios, who was writing c.650 during the Second Messenian War, tell us that the army was organised and fought in three tribes, the Pamphyloi, Hylleis and Dymanes. These tribal names are not traditional. Tribes seem to be a new invention in Homer, where the normal form of politico-military organisation is the warrior-band. It is now thought that the appearance of the tribe represents an 8th century attempt to organise society into more formal structures. If the legends about Lycurgus have any historical value, the three tribes may have been introduced by Lycurgus, perhaps in the mid-8th century and perhaps from Crete, for legends suggest that Lycurgus derived many of his legislative ideas from Cretan practice. If this is so, the Spartan tribe may initially have been divided into *hetaireiai* ('bands of comrades'), as was the case in Crete until the Hellenistic period.

Another subdivision of the tribe mentioned in our sources is the *phratra*, or 'fraternity', a term related to the Latin *frater* (brother). Like the tribe, the *phratra* is now known to be a false kinship group formed to introduce more formal politico-military organisation into aristocratic society; it appears for the first time in Homer. The 27 Spartan *phratrai*, presumably nine were allotted to each tribe, are known to have survived as religious and social clubs which participated in the religious festival of the *Karneia*, religious 'fossils', as it were, of their original military selves. It is known that in 676-673 the poet Terpander was the first ever victor in the poetry competition which formed part of the Karneia. The Karneia must therefore have been introduced, or more probably reformed, at this date. As the *phratrai* are so closely linked with the festival, it is possible that they too were introduced at the same time. Of the total size of the warrior population, we have as yet no idea.

The poet Alkman, who wrote during the last decade of the 7th century, is the first source to mention Sparta's new administrative system of five *obai*, or villages, which replaced the three tribes. Each *oba* supplied one *lochos*, or company, to the army. This reorganisation of the Spartan citizenry into *obai* can be dated to the decades immediately before Alkman. Literary texts also mention two Archaic Spartan organisational structures which, like the *phratrai*, had become 'fossils' in the Classical period – the *enomotia* or 'sworn band', of perhaps 60 men, and the *triakas*, or 'thirty'.

In the tribal system introduced into Athens by Solon in 594 each of the four tribes was divided into 30 *triakades* of 30 men each. If Solon's reforms were based on the Spartan model, then the total warrior population of the five Spartan *lochoi* during this period would have been exactly 4,500 men.

In the Archaic period the Greeks tended to introduce new political and military structures as their population grew. As these new systems were based on exact arithmetic numbers, they only existed in their perfect state for a limited period. They frequently also entailed the enfranchisement of new citizens, as is made clear by the statement of Aristotle *(Pol. 2. 6. 8)* that under the earlier kings, the Spartans used to share their citizenship with others.

Herodotus *(9.10)* informs us that at the battle of Plataea in 479, the five *lochoi* of the Spartan army numbered 5,000. As a thousand cannot be divided by 30, we must assume that the *triakas* had been abandoned as the basic unit of the lockus at some point during the 5th century. In its place we hear of a sub-unit called the *pentekostys* or 'fifty'. One reason for its introduction may have been a demographic expansion of the Spartan population, but it is equally possible that the reform was connected with the start of Sparta's war with Tegea and a political upheaval during the ephorate of Chilon.

Although the *lochos* continued to be the main division of the army until the 5th century, its strength was reduced and its internal structure was changed. Thucydides *(5. 68. 2)* describes the new organisation of the *lochos* in his account of the first battle of Mantineia in 418. The *lochos* of 512 was divided into four *pentekostyes* of 128, and 16 *enomotiai* of 32. Thus the total fighting

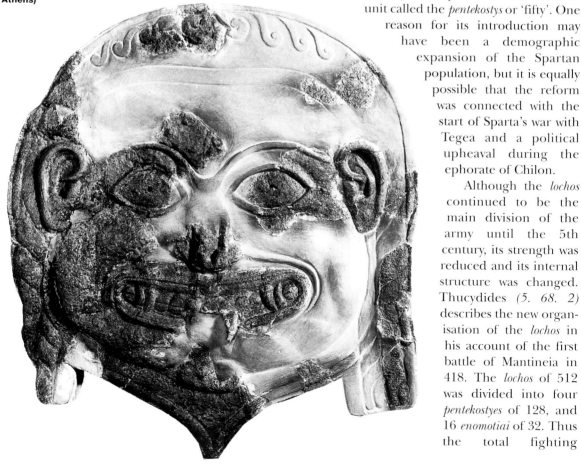

Bronze shield-blazon in the form of a gorgoneion, *c.*530-520, from Sparta. (National Museum Athens)

strength of the Spartiate population had fallen to an establishment strength of 2,560. Several factors may have been influential in this population decline, but the most likely causes are the loss of life in the catastrophic earthquake which hit Sparta around 464 and the losses in battle during the Third Messenian War which followed.

The manpower shortage later became so severe that a new organisational structure was developed in which the *perioikoi* were mixed with the Spartiates. The *mora*, or division, is mentioned for the first time in 403 *(Xen., Hell. 2. 4. 31)*. In two passages Xenophon provides a complete description of the new organisation *(Lac. Pol. 11. 4; Hell. 6. 4. 12)*. The army was now divided into six *morai*, each numbering 576 men, to which were attached 100 cavalry. Thus the total strength of the Lakedaimonian army was now established at 4,056. The *mora*, commanded by a *polemarchos*, was divided into four *lochoi*, eight *pentekostyes* and 16 *enomotiai*. Each *enomotia* now numbered 36 men.

Apart from manpower shortages, which made the inclusion of the *perioikoi* in the new formations imperative, the introduction of the *mora* may also have been influenced by strategic considerations. Starting with the occupation of Dekeleia in Attica in 413, which ultimately proved to be a principal cause of Sparta's victory in the Peloponnesian War, garrisons of Lakedaimonians started to be permanently stationed outside Lakonia. The task of manning these garrisons was rotated between the *morai*. An army organised into five *lochoi*, each recruited from a particular 'village' of Sparta, was no longer desirable, for if disaster should overwhelm one of the garrisons, then the demographic consequences would fall severely on a single territorial division of the city. Consequently, the *oba* was no longer used as the basis of recruitment of the Lakedaimonian army.

Xenophon describes the *mora* in his *Constitution of the Lakedaimonians*, which reached its final form and was published after the battle of Leuktra in 371. We hear nothing more of the *mora* after that battle. Before Leuktra there had been 24 Lakedaimonian *lochoi* in the six *morai*. Descriptions of the Lakedaimonian army from 368 onwards mention that the army was divided into 12 *lochoi*. The internal organisation of the *lochos* is, however, quite uncertain.

Helots and *neodamodeis*

We hear of helots accompanying the army of King Cleomenes in the campaign and battle of Sepeia fought against the Argives in 494. After the battle some of the Argive fugitives took shelter in a sacred grove. Cleomenes ordered all the helots to pile firewood around the grove, and he then set it on fire. In a later incident a local priest attempted to prevent Cleomenes from sacrificing. Cleomenes ordered the helots to pull the priest from the altar and flog him *(Hdt. 6. 80-1)*. Presumably these helots were baggage-carriers, since in all armies it was normal for a hoplite to be accompanied by a slave to carry his baggage. Herodotus *(7. 229)* tells the story of the Spartiate Eurytus at Thermopylae. He had been released from service by Leonidas as an eye infection had blinded him. When he heard of the Persian attack, he asked for his arms and told his helot to take him into the thick of the fighting. The helot did so before running away. Although the practice of each hoplite being accompanied by a helot may have been modified during the later 5th and 4th centuries, we still hear of King Agesilaos being accompanied by his single servant in 362 *(Plut., Vit. Ages. 32. 4)*.

Under exceptional circumstances the Lakedaimonian state also made use of helots as fighters. The army mobilised for the Plataea Campaign of 479 consisted of 5,000 Spartiate hoplites and 35,000 helots (allotted seven to each hoplite) sent out immediately at night, and 5,000 picked hoplites of the *perioikoi* who were assembled and sent out the next day *(Hdt. 9. 10-11)*. It seems reasonably clear that these helots, like the hoplites they accompanied, were recruited from Sparta's own territory. We are later told that of all the *psiloi* (soldiers without heavy armour) accompanying the hoplites of the Greek army, only the helots accompanying the Spartiates were equipped to fight for war. We have no more details of their equipment.

According to Myron of Priene – a Hellenistic author who wrote a historical account of the First Messenian War – the helots were dressed in skin caps and wore an animal skin *(Athen. 14. 657 D)*. Myron interprets this as a deliberately degrading act carried out by the Lakedaimonians upon their serf population. In fact, dress such as this was quite normal for the poorer elements of the Greek agricultural population such as shepherds. It would also have been entirely natural for light-armed troops.

During the Peloponnesian War the Spartans were forced to make increasing use of helot hoplites. We hear of one group of helots sent out to serve with Brasidas in Thrace in 424 and freed upon their return to Lakedaimon in 421. By the time they received their freedom, another group of helot hoplites, the *neodamodeis*, or 'new citizens', had already been freed. Both these groups were given land on the Eleian border at Lepreon *(Thuc. 5. 34. 1)*. These two *lochoi* were later mobilised and fought at the Battle of Mantineia in 418.

We also hear of the periodic use of either *neodamodeis* or of helot hoplites by the Lakedaimonians. Both groups were of servile origin. The *neodamodeis* had already fought in a previous campaign and

Attic tombstone dating to the late 5th century, showing an Athenian hoplite astride his adversary. The latter figure, identified as a Lakedaimonian, seems to wear a *himation* rather than a tunic and a pilos-helmet. Having lost his shield and spear, he defends himself with a short sword. (Metropolitan Museum of Art, New York)

had been freed as a reward. The helot hoplites were new recruits who had not yet completed their service and had been freed. We even hear of helots serving as *harmostai* (governors).

In all cases these helots were presumably Lakonians. The Messenian helots were implacably hostile to the Spartans, as their loss of personal freedom had coincided with loss of national independence. There is no need to suppose that the Lakonian helots would have thought in the same way; they may have been moved to volunteer for military service for patriotic motives as well as the desire to achieve their liberty. Following the disastrous defeat at Leuctra, the Thebans invaded Lakonia. The Spartans proclaimed that any helot who volunteered for service in the war would be freed. No fewer than 6,000 volunteered *(Xen., Hell. 6. 5. 28)*. During their invasion the Thebans captured some helots, presumably some of these volunteers, and ordered them to sing the songs of Terpander, Alkman and Spendon. The helots refused, saying that their masters did not allow it *(Plut., Vit. Lyc. 28. 5)*.

Battle procedure

Xenophon gives details of Spartan battle procedure in chapters 11 to 13 of his *Constitution of the Lakedaimonians*. This forms the basis for the following account.

The army was mobilised by the ephors, who ordered the oldest age-class to be mobilised. While still in Sparta the king sacrificed to 'Zeus Agetor' (Zeus the Leader) and associated gods. If the sacrifice was propitious, the so-called 'fire-bearer' took fire from the altar and led the way to the border, where the king sacrificed to Zeus and Athena before crossing. All the Lakedaimonians were then summoned to the king's tent to hear the poems of Tyrtaios together *(Lycurg., Cont. Leoc. 107)*. The fire-bearer went ahead of the army with the flame from the sacrifice, which was never extinguished. Religious considerations apart, this also ensured that the army had fire to cook with at all times. The fire-bearer would be accompanied by sacrificial animals, including a flock of sheep led by a she-goat called a *katoiadas (Paus. 9. 13. 4)*.

If sacrifice had to be offered in the morning, the king always completed the ceremony before daybreak, so as to be the first to secure the favour of the gods. The sacrifice was attended by the two ephors who accompanied the king on campaign, the *polemarchoi*, *lochagoi* and *pentekosteres*, the commanders *(stratiarchai)* of the various mercenary detachments, the commanders of the baggage train, and any of the commanders of the allied contingents who wished to be present. When the sacrifice was over, the king gave his orders of the day to the senior officers present.

An organised orders chain existed. Thucydides *(5. 66)* tells us how at the First Battle of Mantineia, King Agis gave his orders to the *polemarchoi*; these in turn gave orders to the *lochagoi*; then they to the *pentekosteres*; and they to the *enomotarchai*, who finally informed the whole *enomotia* of what was to be done. In 418 orders were clearly given in a top-down hierarchy. It seems the system changed with the introduction of the *mora*. In 395 Pausanias appeared in Boeotia with an army from Lakedaimon, and upon hearing of the death of Lysander at Haliartos, he called together the *polemarchoi* and the *pentekosteres* (*cf. Xen, Hell. 3. 5. 22*). Likewise, in 390, upon hearing of the annihilation of a

Lakedaimonian *mora* by the Athenian general Iphicrates at Lechaion, Agesilaos called together the *polemarchoi*, the *pentekosteres* and the commanders of the allied contingents *(Xen., Hell. 4. 5. 7)*. So the four *lochagoi* in each *mora* and the 16 *enomotarchai* remained in the ranks to keep control.

On the march the king led the army, preceded only by the Skiritai and a cavalry screen. He decided when to stop to camp, and selected the campsite. The army encamped in a circle and guards were posted, with some watching the camp, in case of treachery by allies or slaves. Cavalry pickets were posted on high ground to watch for the enemy, and these were guarded by Skiritai at night.

The army was ordered to engage in athletic exercises while on campaign, and this took place both in the morning and in the evening when in camp. After morning exercises were finished the senior *polemarchos* had the herald give the order to sit down and the men were reviewed. They then took breakfast and relieved the outposts. The signal for going to evening meal was also given by the army herald *(Hdt. 6. 77-8)*. After the army had finished dinner, they sang a hymn. Then each man in turn sang something by Tyrtaios. The *polemarchos* acted as the

Lakedaimonian warrior shown on an early Apulian calyx-crater by '*the Painter of the Berlin Dancing Girl*' dating to about 420. Note the two locks falling over the shoulder, the long beard and the shaven upper lip. He holds his spear, nearly nine feet long, close to the butt-spike, to keep the native cavalryman at bay. The shield has a bronze reinforcing band on the inside of the bronze rim. This secures a handle for the left hand, attached to the rim, and two arm-straps, allowing the shield to be carried on the back. (Wellesley College Museum, Wellesley, Mass, USA) judge and gave a prize of meat to the winner *(Athen. 630 F)*. The men then rested by their arms.

The army slept in groups of *syskenoi*, or 'tent-companions'. Xenophon *(Hell. 7. 1. 15-16)* tells us of a Theban attack on a Lakedaimonian camp when the night watches were coming to an end and the men were rising from their camp-beds and going to wherever each one had to go; it seems that the army 'stood-to' in the morning.

The Lakedaimonians had prescribed procedures for pitched battle. When the opposing armies had closed to a few hundred metres – near enough for the enemy to be seen clearly – it was the Lakedaimonian practice to sacrifice a female goat to Artemis Agrotera, the goddess of the chase *(Xen., Hell. 4. 2. 20)*. The king then commanded every Lakedaimonian to put on a wreath, and ordered the many pipers in the ranks to play the hymn to Castor. The king would then start singing one of the marching-songs of Tyrtaios, and the pipers would take up the tune. As the hoplite line moved forward, the Lakedaimonians kept in step by singing these marching-songs to the accompaniment of the pipes *(Athen. 14. 627 D, 630 E)*. As Thucydides explained *(5. 71)*, this custom had no religious motive but was done 'in order that they may advance in line, keeping good time, that their ranks might not be broken, a thing which great armies often do as they close with the enemy'. The Greek pipe or flute cannot be compared to modern instruments of that name. It had a lower and more powerful sound, similar to the oboe or bassoon. The posts of army herald, piper, and cook were inherited *(Hdt. 6. 60)*. In camp, orders would be given by the herald, but in battle, because of the noise, signals were ggiven by trumpet. We hear, for example, of a signal for withdrawal *(Diod. 15. 34. 1)*.

Normally the two lines would not meet. Such was the reputation of the Lakedaimonians that their enemies rarely stood their ground. If they did, a desperate fight ensued, and the discipline of the Lakedaimonians generally enabled them to win. In the 5th century, however, when armies fought in alliances, the Lakedaimonian victory might only be local – in their place of honour on the right wing. So the Lakedaimonians developed new tactics: having achieved a local victory, they wheeled their line round to face left and began to roll up the enemy line by attacking it in flank.

Persons accused of cowardice were excluded from holding any office and banned from making any legally binding contract. Any citizen

The inside of this Lakonian cup, decorated by the 'Hunt Painter' – named after the hunt scene painted on another of his cups – c.550-540, shows two young warriors carrying a dead warrior from the battlefield. Note the hairstyles. (Antikensammlung, Staatliche Museen zu Berlin, Preussischer Kulturbsitz) could strike them with impunity. They were forced to wear cloaks with coloured patches and to shave off half their beards, and no citizen would give them a woman in marriage. Punishments were devised for lesser military offences. For example, insubordination was punished by extra sentry duty, which meant carrying a heavy shield throughout the night.

DRESS

In ancient Greece the two sexes lived largely separate lives. Males would spend much of the day in the fields, females around the house. Representations show, and texts describe, men doing dirty work like ploughing, sowing or potting naked. Athletic nudity may have been ritual in origin. At the start of the Archaic period light clothes were worn during athletic exercise, but they were eventually discarded completely. The rigours of warfare – marching and fighting in heavy armour often under the summer sun – were hardly less demanding than those of sport and physical training. Nor was warfare of less ritual significance than sport. When we see representations of Spartans fighting without a tunic, we should not dismiss them as being 'artistic' or 'heroising': undoubtedly some are, but nudity in Greek art is, more often than not, a depiction of reality.

Lakonian bronze figurine of a warrior from Dodona. (Ioannina Museum)

Crimson clothing

According to Xenophon *(Lac. Pol. 11. 3),* Lycurgus had ordered the Lakedaimonians to wear a crimson robe and a bronze shield because the robe least resembled women's clothing and was most warlike, and the shield could be polished quickly but tarnished slowly. Later sources expand on Xenophon's explanations. Plutarch *(Mor. 238 F)* noted that the blood-coloured tunic aroused terror in the inexperienced opponent and helped disguise wounds. When Xenophon was writing, it had become virtually universal for Greek armies to dress in crimson, largely as a result of Lakedaimonian influence, so his statement that crimson is a warlike colour makes perfect sense for the 4th century. The real reason, however, seems to lie elsewhere.

In antiquity the production of clothes by hand was time-consuming and costly. Most clothes were produced within the household. Although our knowledge is somewhat sketchy, it seems that right down to the end of the 5th century many people owned only one cloak, and it was normal to borrow a cloak from the neighbour when yours was being cleaned. The situation probably changed later on, but most people would own a limited range of clothes. Xenophon *(An. 3. 2. 7)* tells us that he wore his finest clothes for battle, for, if the gods granted victory, it was appropriate to be wearing one's best clothes to mark the occasion, or if he should die, it was also fitting to meet one's fate well attired. These feelings seem to have been widely held.

One imagines that the wives and mothers of the Spartan warriors would have wished to produce tunics of the finest quality for their men folk who were about to risk their life in battle, and crimson may have come into general use because it was an expensive dye. The uniformity of crimson could have arisen from general practice and only later been sanctioned by formal legislation. How far back the custom of wearing crimson clothing for military service actually went cannot be established, although it could have been an early practice (see Plate B). The warrior bronzes of the early 5th century continue to show highly decorated tunics, so even if the wearing of crimson had become formalised by that date, it is still a long way away from standardised dress. In the 4th century the army of Agesilaos was clad entirely in crimson. By this time it seems appropriate to talk of uniform military dress, which may sometimes have been issued by a commander. Crimson had become the colour of the soldier and especially of the Lakedaimonian soldier. The Lakedaimonian was even buried in his crimson robe *(Plut., Vit. Lyc. 27. 1)*.

The tunic

The basic item of clothing was the tunic *(chiton)*. In the Archaic period tunics were relatively thick woollen garments, but in the Classical period they became lighter, and sometimes linen replaced wool. During the 5th century a new type of tunic, called the *exomis*, came into widespread use. Originally the *exomis* was typically used by workmen to allow free movement of the right arm. Once the cuirass had been abandoned, in the 5th century, the Lakedaimonians adopted the new tunic for warfare. The *exomis* tunic was two-sleeved, but the right-hand sleeve of the tunic could be let down to leave the right shoulder and arm free to handle weapons when in combat. This is what is described by Plutarch in his *Life of Cleomenes (37. 2)*. The Hellenistic king Cleomenes III of Sparta put on his tunic and loosened the seam from his right shoulder. The seam was presumably pinned back in place when the wearer wished to wear the *exomis* with the sleeve covering the right shoulder. Over time, the crimson *exomis* was adopted by armies imitating Lakedaimonian military practices, and by individuals imitating the Lakedaimonian lifestyle in general.

The cloak

The Greeks distinguished between two types of cloak, the *himation* and the *chlamys*. Both were rectangular, but the *himation* was much longer and was worn wrapped round the body. The *chlamys* was draped over the left shoulder and secured by a pin over the right shoulder. The *himation* was much favoured in the Archaic period, but was largely replaced in the Classical period by the *chlamys*, which was much looser and more suitable for travelling, hunting and other activities which required greater freedom of movement. The

Grave stele of Lisas the Tegean, a member of the Peloponnesian garrison installed at Dekeleia in 413. He wears an *exomis* tunic (note the sleeve lying below his right arm) and a pilos-helmet in the Lakedaimonian style. *(Bulletin de Correspondence Hellénique 4, 1880)*

chlamys was normally worn over a tunic, the *himation* without an undergarment.

The Lakedaimonians retained their traditional form of *himation* throughout the Classical period, and it was never replaced by the *chlamys*. The cloak was not normally worn in battle, but off-duty and in peacetime. Like other items of dress used by the Lakedaimonians, the cloak was dyed crimson. When the earthquake of 464 killed a huge number of Spartans, and the helots were threatening to revolt, the Spartans sent Perikleidas to beg for help in Athens, where he sat 'as pale as death in his crimson cloak' *(Arist., Lys. 1140)*.

The Lakedaimonian *himation* was called a *triboμn*. In Greek texts the *triboμn* is often described as being *phaulos* (mean), which is often translated as 'short'. In fact, representations show it to have been long but thin. Boys under training had to wear the same cloak in winter and summer in order to become accustomed to the cold *(Xen., Lac. Pol. 2. 4)*. Adults also wore the thin cloak all year round to show their physical toughness. Agesilaos is mentioned as wearing only a cloak during the winter of 362 *(Plut., Vit. Ages. 32. 4)*. It even became a popular fashion to leave the cloak unwashed in order to show that the wearer had only one cloak which he wore for the whole year. Along with other distinctive items of Lakedaimonian dress, the *triboμn* was adopted abroad by individuals who admired the Lakedaimonians and aped their lifestyles. In particular, the philosophers and their disciples in Athens keenly adopted the *triboun*.'. Xenophon *(Mem. 1. 6. 2)* described Socrates as dressed in a thin cloak 'in winter and summer alike'. Aristophanes *(Birds 1281-3)* described Lakonian-mad young men as 'long-haired, hungry, unwashed, Socrates-like, carrying sticks'.

Shoes

It is frequently claimed that it was an artistic convention to show the foot bare in Greek art. This belief is based on ignorance of the literary sources. Physical work out of doors was generally performed barefoot. The normal Greek soldier was a farmer who worked barefoot in the fields, took his physical exercise barefoot, and so saw no need to don footwear when called upon to perform military service. Boots were worn for specific purposes, such as for hunting, where the hunter was likely to have to run through prickly undergrowth. Soldiers did wear boots in the winter, but for warmth rather than for protection. The standard type of boot took the form of a leather strapwork frame holding *piloi*, or felt socks, in place against the leg. When texts mention soldiers barefoot, they generally do so in a context where troops have been overtaken by winter while dressed in their summer clothing (eg. *Xen., Hell. 2.1.1*). Plato *(Laws 1. 633 B)* informs us that the Lakedaimonians went barefoot even in the winter while serving in the *krypteia*. Boys were forbidden to wear shoes lest their feet became soft *(Xen., Lac. Pol. 2.3)*. Consequently, in our reconstructions we should no more give shoes to Greek soldiers than fig-leaves to Greek athletes.

Even so, we do hear of a special type of Lakonian shoe. Literary sources describe it as being single-soled (*haplai*). Demosthenes *(54. 34)* referred to 'those who Lakonize with their *triboμnes* and single-soled footwear'. Consequently, we can identify the open-toed sandal with a ongue at the top, on statues of Greek philosophers, as the Lakonian shoe. Pollux *(Onom. 7. 88)* informed us that the shoe was coloured red (not crimson).

The Lakonian staff

Our sources also mention a distinctive Lakedaimonian staff (*bakteμrion*). Theophrastus *(Char. 21. 15)* tells us they were 'crooked' or 'aslant', but we get no other clues from literary sources as to their shape . A number of different types of staff are found in Greek art – rough, smooth, curved, straight, with a crook at the top or a cross-piece. Fortunately, a single Spartan representation of a man with a staff has survived. The staff is long, smooth, straight and has a T-shaped cross-piece at the top. This type of staff is also depicted being used by philo-Lakonian philosophers.

Although the Lakedaimonian staff was not a weapon of war, it was carried by Sparta's representatives abroad, such as generals, envoys or military governors (*harmostai*). The staff and the *triboμn* became, as it were, symbols of the majesty of Sparta, as Plutarch *(Vit. Nic. 19. 4)* refers to them, in his account of the despatch of Gylippus to Sicily. When Athens fell, at the end of the Peloponnesian War, Lysander put a garrison into the Acropolis and appointed the Spartan Kallibios as *harmosteμs.* We are told that Kallibios once lifted his staff to strike

Bronze plaque from Pompeii showing Socrates wearing a *triboμn* and leaning on a Lakedaimonian *bakteμrion*. (*Römische Mitteilungen* 55, 1940)

Autolukos the athlete, upon which Autolukos siezed him by the legs and threw him to the ground *(Plut., Vit Lys. 15. 5)*.

Hairstyles

Xenophon *(Lac. Pol. 11. 3)* tells us that men who had entered manhood were permitted to wear their hair long, in the belief that it made them look taller, more dignified and more terrifying. According to another version, long hair made handsome men more beautiful and ugly men more terrible *(Plut., Vit. Lys. 1. 2; Mor. 189 E, 228 F)*. In antiquity, a legend existed which said that legislation enjoining the Lakedaimonians to grow their hair, contrary to previous practice, had first been instituted after the Battle of the Champions *(Hdt. 1. 82. 8)*, and according to Aristotle *(Rhet. 1. 9. 26)*, the Lakedaimonians thought long hair noble because it was the mark of a free man, since it is difficult to perform any servile tasks with long hair. In fact the Lakedaimonians wore their hair long because in Archaic times long hair was the mark of an aristocrat. Its retention was a symptom of the increasing conservatism of Lakedaimonian society from the middle of the 6th century. Outside Lakedaimon, long hair became a sign of Lakonian sympathies.

Early 6th century limestone relief in Sparta Museum (1482) from the sanctuary of Artemis Orthia in Sparta. Note the Lakedaimonian staff carried by the man. (Maria Pipili, *Laconian Iconography of the 6th century BC,* 1987)

The Lakonian hairstyle did change somewhat over time. On warrior statuettes of the 5th century all the locks are swept to the back under the helmet. In the early 4th century, hair is normally dressed in four locks falling to the front, two on either shoulder, and four to the back. The beard is short and pointed and the upper lip is normally shaven. Plutarch *(Vit. Cleom. 9. 3)*, quoting Aristotle, informs us that every year upon entering office the ephors would order the citizens to 'cut their moustaches and obey the law'. In the later 5th century, it seems that the hair continued to be dressed in two locks to the front on either shoulder, and the upper lip continued to be shaved, but the beard was generally worn longer. Plutarch *(Vit. Lys. 1. 1)* confirms this when he describes the statue of Lysander in the treasury of the Acanthians at Delphi as having very long hair and beard 'in the old style'. Plutarch *(Mor. 232 E)* preserves a saying of a Lakonian who, upon being asked why he wore his beard so very long, said: 'So I can see my grey hairs and never do anything unworthy of them'. In the 4th century both hair and beard may have been cut shorter.

An indispensable piece of equipment for any self-respecting Lakedaimonian was his comb. When Clearchus, the Spartan general who commanded the 10,000 Greek mercenaries under Cyrus the Younger, was captured by trick, he was sent to the Persian court in chains. There he begged a comb from the Greek court physician Ktesias. He was so pleased at being able to comb his hair, he gave Ktesias his ring *(Plut., Vit. Artax. 18. 1)*.

Miniature comb, probably dedicated by a child, from the sanctuary of Artemis Orthia in Sparta. The purpose of the hole was probably to allow the comb to be hung on a peg. The teeth are missing. (Oxford, Ashmolean Museum)

HOPLITE WEAPONRY

Plutarch *(Vit. Ages. 34. 7-8)* tells us that during the surprise attack made on Sparta by the Theban general Epaminondas in 362, Isidas (son of Phoibidas) fought naked in the battle, without armour or clothing, for he had just anointed his body. He ran out of his house grabbing a sword and spear, and rushed directly to the fight. He emerged from the battle without a scratch. After the battle the ephors crowned him with a wreath for his courage and fined him a thousand drachmas for risking his life in battle without armour, presumably against regulations. Weaponry that was to be carried into battle may also have been specified.

Spear

The main offensive weapon of the Spartan hoplite was his spear. King Agesilaos used to say that the walls of Sparta were its young men, and its borders the points of their spears *(Plut., Mor. 217 E)*. On campaign, the Lakedaimonian hoplite was ordered to carry his spear at all times *(Xen., Lac. Pol. 12. 4)*. The wood which the Greeks normally chose for their spear-shafts was ash. Tyrtaios *(frg. 19. 13)* confirms that the Lakedaimonians used ash. The long, straight grain of ash allows the seasoned trunk of a felled tree to be split into longer and straighter sections than most other woods. The same qualities make ash the wood which best combines lightness and strength. From the start, the spear-head seems to have been made of iron and leaf-shaped. Only later did the spear acquire a bronze butt-spike, which allowed the spear to be fixed in the ground when weapons were piled up, without damaging the shaft or exposing it to rot through contact with the damp earth.

Bronze spear-head found in a pit in Building I in the Sanctuary of Zeus Messapeus located at Tsakona, near Sparta. It is either Archaic or early Classical in date. (British School at Athens 85, 1990)

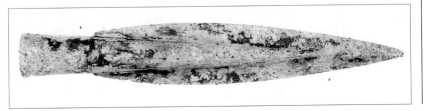

Shield

Many know the anecdote preserved by Plutarch *(Mor. 241 F)* that one Spartan mother when handing her son his shield before battle admonished him to return 'either with it or on it'. After the spear, the shield was the most important item of hoplite equipment. Warriors who threw away their shields were severely punished. When someone asked the exiled Spartan king Demaratos *(r. 510-491)* why people who lost their shields were dishonoured but those who lost their helmets or cuirasses were not, he replied: 'Because the latter they put on for their own protection, but the shield for the common good of the whole line.' *(Plut., Mor. 220 A)* This passage also, incidentally, confirms that the cuirass was still being worn during the Persian Wars.

Of all the elements in the hoplite panoply, the hoplite shield appeared the latest – around 700. Until then the Dipylon shield had been the most popular type. The hoplite shield was made of small segments of wood glued together and faced with layers of leather. It was circular and slightly dish-shaped in section, with an offset rim around the edge. This rim was covered by a thin layer of bronze, usually decorated with a 'guilloche' (cable) pattern. The shield was held by two handles. In the middle of the shield was a bronze arm-hole (*porpax*) through which the left arm was passed as far as the elbow. Normally this arm-hole was incorporated into a long bronze band stretching to either edge of the shield. Critias tells us that the Lakedaimonians used to remove the *porpax* from their shields when stored at home as a precaution against them being stolen and used by helots in the event of a revolt. The left hand gripped a leather or rope handle (*antilabe μ*) which was fixed to the rim of the shield. Sometimes a bronze shield device was fixed to the front of the shield, and sometimes there were reinforcing plates, possibly of bronze, on the inside of the shield, behind the forearm and shoulder. A number of possible Lakedaimonian bronze shield devices have been identified, the latest of which dates to *c.*530-520.

A fundamental change, apparently first noted by Philip Henry Blyth, took place in the construction of the hoplite shield shortly before the end of the 6th century. The whole shield was covered by a thin sheet of stressed bronze, and the profile of the shield took on a much deeper, bowed shape. At the same time, the wooden or leather sub-structure of the shield may have been laminated and stressed for strength.

The only evidence we have for the issue of equipment is a reference to horsemen being given their equipment on mobilisation prior to the battle of Leuktra in 371 *(Xen., Hell. 6. 4. 11)*. Nevertheless (and especially when the Lakedaimonians started to use a uniform city shield blazon), shields would have been virtually identical. It was Lakedaimonian practice to pile arms when at rest on campaign *(Hdt. 7. 208-9)*, and it must have been difficult to identify one's own shield quickly unless they were marked with the name of the owner.

At first the shield was decorated with the owner's individual shield

ABOVE **Bronze butt-spike from Olympia. The inscription tells us that it was dedicated by the Messenians as booty taken from the Lakedaimonians. The dedication seems to date to the troubled period of the 460s. (© German Archaeological Institute, Athens)**

RIGHT **Excavations in the Athenian Agora have unearthed a shield whose inscription states that it is one of the shields captured from the Lakedaimonians at Pylos in 425. Pausanias *(1. 15. 4)* notes that the shields captured at Pylos were kept in the Painted Stoa, smeared in pitch for preservation. The shield was badly crushed, and in its present state has a diameter of between 83 and 95cm. Note the guilloche pattern on the rim. (American School of Classical Studies at Athens, Agora Excavations).**

device. Plutarch *(Mor. 234 D)* tells us that one Lakonian had a life-size fly as his shield emblem. When someone said that he had done this to escape being noticed, he replied that it was rather that he may be noticeable, for he would come so close to the enemy, they would notice it at its true size. At some point, possibly *c.*475-450, the Lakedaimonians began to use a uniform state shield device.

In the Lexicon of Photius, under the entry for the letter Λ *(lambda)*, we are told that the Lakedaimonians painted this letter on their shields. Photius mentions as his source Eupolis, an Athenian comic poet born in 446. His last known drama was staged in 412, and he died "in the

Hellespont", probably at the battle of Kynossema in 411. Therefore it is certain that the *lambda* shield device was in use before 412, and it is generally thought that this fragment of Eupolis comes from a comedy dealing with the Mantineia campaign of 418. The letter was presumably painted onto the shield in the uniform crimson colour. The use of the *lambda* continued into the 3rd century, when we are told that some Messenian troops managed to seize Elis by trick, having painted Lakonian badges onto their shields *(Paus. 4. 28. 5)*.

Cuirass

The type of cuirass in use throughout the Archaic period is distinguished by an offset flange at the waist, giving it a shape resembling the flaring mouth of a bell. Hence archaeologists call it the 'bell' cuirass. On earlier examples of the bell type, the musculature is only sketchily imitated by chasing. Later, the partially modelled musculature is sometimes part covered with ornate decoration. By the early 5th century the musculature is fully modelled, but the flange at the waist has not yet been abandoned. In the early 5th century the bell cuirass evolved into the 'muscle' cuirass.

The bronze 'muscle' cuirass was closely modelled to the musculature of the body. Instead of having a flange at the bottom, it curves up at the sides to allow free movement to the hips, and down over the abdomen to afford some protection to the groin. The 'composite' cuirass, with its tie-down shoulder pieces and segmented body-armour, does not seem to have been worn by the Lakedaimonians at any time, at least, it does not appear among the surviving representations. It must be admitted, however, that we are dealing with a rather small sample of evidence.

At some point during the 5th century, possibly *c.*450-425, the Lakedaimonian army decided to discard their cuirasses. Behind this move seems to have been a search for battlefield mobility as well as the need for rapid marching on campaign. In due course other Greek armies followed the Lakedaimonian lead and abandoned their heavy body armour. This situation continued into the 360s, when representational evidence indicates that the cuirass was adopted again. This change may be associated with new battlefield tactics introduced by the Theban general Epaminondas.

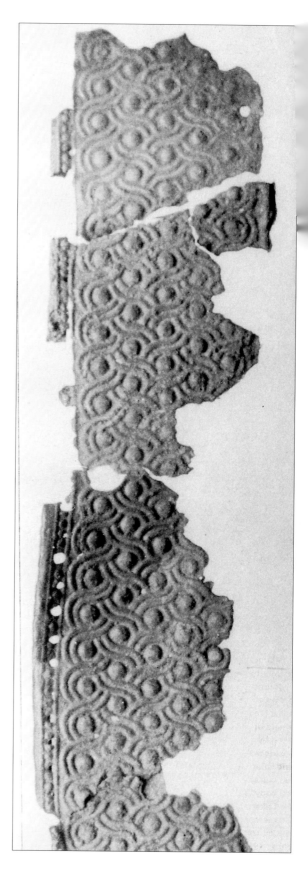

Helmet

After the shield, the most important piece of hoplite armour was the helmet. In the Archaic period the most popular type in Sparta, as in the rest of Greece, was the Corinthian helmet, which was being produced by 700. The helmet completely enclosed the head, and, though vision and hearing were restricted, the protection offered was especially valued in the spear-fighting of hoplite warfare. Other more open-faced types also seem to have been used by the Lakedaimonians.

When Lakedaimonian battlefield tactics started to develop in the 5th century, the Corinthian helmet was replaced. Good vision and hearing in the phalanx were becoming more important as increasingly complex

It is known that Archidamus III, born between 408 and 400, was honoured with statues at Olympia and Delphi. This portrait bust, presumably a Roman copy of one of these statues, is identified by a painted inscription. It portrays the King aged about 40, and so around the year 360. If the cuirass is not an addition by the copyist, it demonstrates that the Lakedaimonians re-adopted the cuirass in the 360s. (A. Hekler, *Greek and Roman Portraits*, 1912)

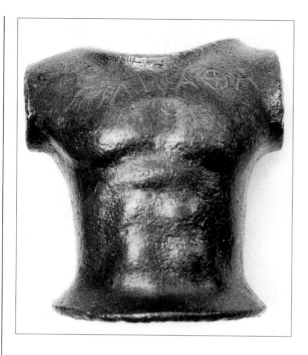

manoeuvres were executed at the signal of the trumpet. Consequently, a new type of helmet, the pilos-helmet, was adopted at the same time as the cuirass was abandoned.

The word *pilos* literally means 'felt', and is applied to a number of articles made of that material. Felt caps were called *piloi*, and they came in a number of regional variants, distinguished by shape. Lakonian *piloi* are mentioned by Arrian *(Tact. 3. 5)* and Pollux *(1. 149)*. They were conical in shape and slightly rounded at the point – of the type worn by the Lakedaimonian heroes Castor and Polydeukes (Pollux). Hats of this shape were also popular in the Dorian colonies in the Greek west, some founded by Sparta itself. The pilos-helmet repeated the shape of the felt *pilos* cap in bronze. Presumably *pilos* caps were sometimes worn under the helmet for comfort, giving rise to helmets of this shape. Once adopted by the Lakedaimonian army, it became as much a Lakonian symbol as the crimson *exomis*, and was copied by many armies both inside and outside the Peloponnesian League.

A famous passage in Thucydides *(4. 34. 3)* has provoked considerable discussion. It tells us that the Spartan garrison on the islet of Sphacteria suffered greatly against Athenian archers, 'for their *piloi* did not keep out the arrows'. Thucydides may be suggesting that the Spartans were wearing felt *piloi*, but it is more probable that by this time the word *pilos* was also used to refer to bronze helmets of that type. It seems that the pilos-helmet continued to be used by the Lakedaimonians to the end of the Classical period, despite it being replaced by more enclosed types in many other armies.

Bronze miniature bell cuirass from the Spartan Acropolis. The retrograde inscription across the chest informs us that the votive has been dedicated to Athena. (Sparta Museum)

Pilos-helmet from the Carapanos Collection (687), presumably from Dodona. (National Museum Athens)

Other body armour

The legs were protected by bronze greaves, clipped onto the shins and held in place by the springiness of the metal. In the 7th century greaves were rather short, reaching up the shin as far as the knee but leaving the knee itself unprotected. In the 6th century the greave first extends upwards to cover the knee, and then by the end of the century it also extends far enough down to partially cover the ankle. As one of the most easily discarded items of body armour, greaves were abandoned in the late 5th century search for tactical mobility.

During the middle decades of the 6th century, further items of body-armour were added to the Greek panoply, attested either by actual examples or in representations. They include upper and lower arm-guards for the right arm, which was unprotected by the hoplite shield, thigh-guards, ankle-guards and foot- or toe-guards. That these items were in use in the Spartan army too is attested by the Lakonian warrior-statuette from Longa. Depiction of supplementary items of body-armour grows in Greek vase-painting until about 530-525, and then it suddenly stops. The reason may have been the growth of Persian power: Lydia fell in 546, Babylonia in 539, Egypt in 525, and in 523 Polycrates, the powerful tyrant of Samos, was captured and put to death by the Persians. War between the states of mainland Greece and the Persians became increasingly likely, and the hoplite had to develop new tactics to counter massed archery. The strategy adopted by the hoplite phalanx was to charge the enemy at a run, so minimising the time they were exposed to archers. The Greeks charged the Persian line in this way at both Marathon and Plataea. An athletic competition, the *hoplitodromos*, or 'armed race', was developed to train citizens in this new military manoeuvre. It was introduced into the Olympic Games in 520 and into the Delphic in 498. Clearly there was no room for supplementary body armour in these changed tactical conditions.

The sword

There was nothing unusual in Lakedaimonian swords until the 5th century, when they began to get shorter. By *c.*425-400 they had become exceedingly short, like daggers, as is testified to by numerous literary passages. When one Athenian mocked that the Lakonian swords were so short a juggler could swallow them, King Agis III replied *(r. 338-331)* : 'But nevertheless we still strike our enemies with them,' *(Plut., Vit. Lyc. 19. 2; Mor. 191 E)* King Agesilaos, when asked why the Lakedaimonian swords were so short, replied: "Because we fight close to the enemy." *(Plut., Mor. 217 E, 232 E)*. Finally, a Spartan woman, when her son complained that his sword was too small, advised him to add a step forward to it *(Plut., Mor. 241 F)*.

The sword was probably shortened to make it handier in the crush which ensued when the two phalanx lines met. Normal Greek swords were medium-sized cut and thrust weapons. When the spear was broken, they would normally be used overhand to slash at the head of the opponent. The sword was shortened in order to encourage the Lakedaimonian warrior to use more effective thrusting attacks at the trunk and groin of his opponent. Such attacks would have been especially effective when the armies opposing the Lakedaimons had started to discard their body armour too.

No example of the short Lakonian sword has survived. However, this bronze model of a sword, purchased in Crete in 1898, may well reproduce the shape. At 32.2cm long it is slightly larger than life-size and made of solid bronze, and so is probably best interpreted as a bronze fitting for a slightly larger-than-life statue of a warrior. (Trustees of the British Museum)

Ancillary equipment

A description of the Spartan drinking mug (*kothon*) has been preserved by Plutarch *(Vit. Lyc. 9. 4)*. It was valued highly for its usefulness among soldiers on active service. Its colour hid the disagreeable appearance of the water which they were often forced to drink, and its curving lip caught the muddy sediment and held it inside, so that only the purer part of the water reached the mouth of the drinker. Suidas *(s.v.)* adds the information that the Lakonian *kothon* was one-handled. Athenaeus preserves the description of Kritias: the lips were curved and served to trap any foreign bodies in the water. It was most easily carried in a *gylios*. The *gylios* is mentioned in the comedies of Aristophanes *(Acharn. 1097)*, and an ancient commentator on this passage tells us that it was a wicker-work basket in which soldiers put their provisions on campaign.

Each soldier would probably also have carried his *xule*, or whittling knife. The Greek verb *xuo* means 'to scrape', so a spear which had been shaved smooth was called a *xyston* and the implement used was called a *xuele*. Thus a spear-maker was called a 'spear-whittler' *(Pollux 1. 149)*. In his *Cyropaedia (6. 2. 32)*, Xenophon has his imaginary Cyrus recommend that his soldiers should carry medicines, plenty of straps, a file for sharpening the spearhead, and also a *xuele*, if they knew how to use one. It is quite possible that Xenophon is recommending that Lakedaimonian practice be followed here. Xenophon *(An. 4. 8. 26)* mentions that a Spartiate named Drakontios, who took part in the 'Expedition of the Ten Thousand', had been exiled from Sparta as a boy because he had accidentally killed another boy with a stroke of his *xuele*. Perhaps the Spartiates were taught to whittle new spear-shafts as part of their military training during boyhood. It seems that the Lakonian *xuele*, or rather *xuale* in Lakonian dialect, was distinguished by its length, for Xenophon *(An. 4. 7. 16)* tells us that the Chalybians carried a sword as big as a Lakonian *xuele* and used it to decapitate their prisoners.

Finally the hoplite or his helot had to carry equipment for cooking and eating. In 390, during campaigning around Corinth, we are told *(Xen., Hell. 4. 5. 4)* that Agesilaos won great credit among his soldiers for his thoughtfulness. One hoplite *mora* had been sent to occupy a mountain and spend the night there, dressed only in summer clothing. Rain and hail fell, and when they started to prepare their meal, it turned out that not one of those carrying food for the *mora* had brought fire with them. This passage shows that on operations away from the main army, the hoplites would not be accompanied by a helot each, but only by enough helots to carry their food. It further implies that rations were issued to the troops by this date. To avoid a collapse in morale, Agesilaos sent the *mora* ten men carrying fire in *chytrai*, or earthenware cooking pots. The morale of the men was raised greatly by the fires. The soldiers anointed themselves with oil before eating their dinner. This tells us that they carried an *aryballos* (oil-flask) to anoint themselves, and presumably a strigil to scrape away the surplus oil and dirt. On this occasion cooking

Lakonian drinking mug from Tocra. (J. Boardman, J. Hayes, *Excavations at Tocra 1963-1965,* **The Archaic Deposits I,1966)**

WARRIORS IN THE AGE OF LYCURGUS
1: Warrior with cuirass and Dipylon shield
2: Warrior with bronze belt and Dipylon shield
3: Warrior with Herzsprung shield

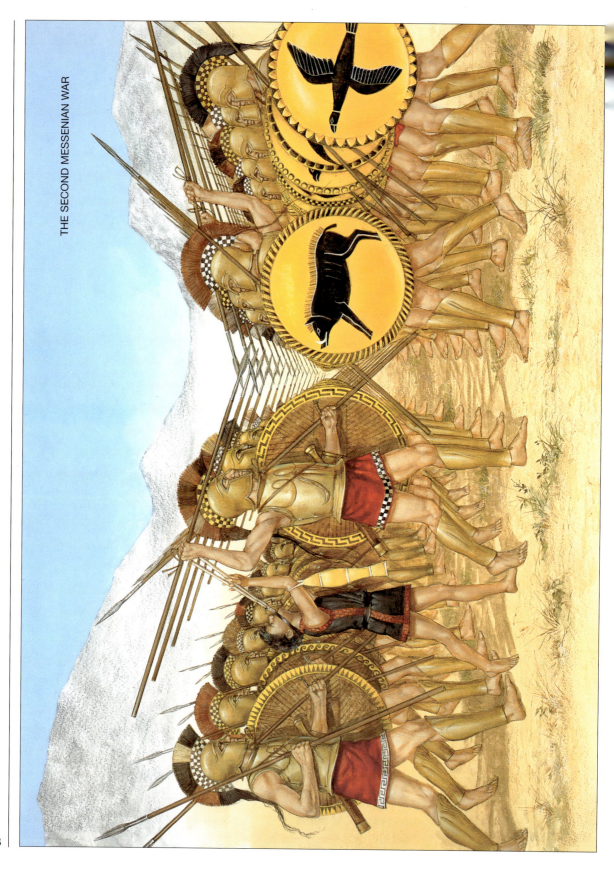

THE SPARTAN KINGS, EARLY 6th CENTURY
1: Spartan king
showing inside
of shield
2: Spartan king
showing outside
of shield
3: Hoplite with
scalloped-cheek
helmet

C

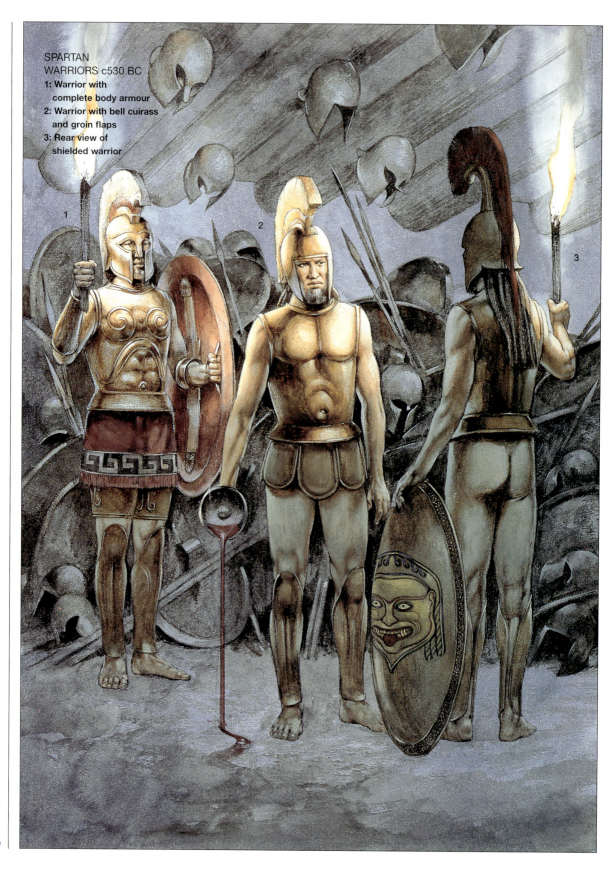

SPARTAN
WARRIORS c530 BC
1: Warrior with
   complete body armour
2: Warrior with bell cuirass
   and groin flaps
3: Rear view of
   shielded warrior

D

THE BATTLE OF THERMOPYLAE, 480 BC

AMOMPHARETOS AT THE
BATTLE OF PLATAEA, 479 BC
1: Athenian herald
2: Pausanias
3: Euryanax
4: Amompharetos

F

SPARTAN ARMY, c.470 BC
1: Spartan hoplite
2: Spartan piper
3: Spartan trumpeter

G

THE FIRST BATTLE OF MANTINEIA, 418 BC
1: Lakedaimonian hoplite
2: Lakedaimonian junior officer
3: Lakedaimonian senior
   commander

LYSANDER'S FLEET AT AIGOSPOTAMOI, 405 BC
1: Megarian steersman
2: Allied hoplite marine
3: Naval archer

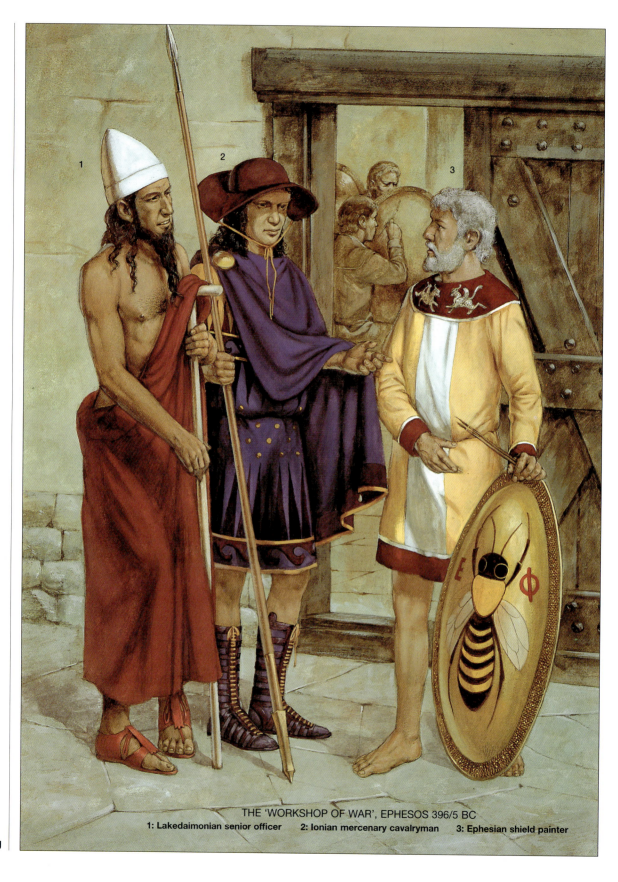

THE 'WORKSHOP OF WAR', EPHESOS 396/5 BC
1: Lakedaimonian senior officer   2: Ionian mercenary cavalryman   3: Ephesian shield painter

MERCENARY INFANTRY REGIMENTS
1: Cyrean mercenary   2: Derkylidas mercenary   3: Greek mercenary archer

K

SKIRMISH NEAR TANAGRA, 377 BC
1: Lakedaimonian cavalryman
2: Skiritan soldier
3: Theban hoplite

L

was presumably carried out communally, but on other occasions it may have been carried out individually by the hoplite's helot. Each hoplite must, however, have carried a plate to eat from and presumably each helot carried a *chytra*.

OTHER ARMS

Cavalry

Following their victory at Pylos in 42, the Athenians established raiding bases at Pylos and on the island of Kythera. In response to this dangerous military threat, the Lakedaimonians decided, contrary to their earlier military practices, to raise a force of 400 cavalry and some archers *(Thuc. 4. 55. 2)*. This decision – a good one from a military point of view – stretched the finances of a state which scarcely possessed a monetary economy at the time. Xenophon *(Hell. 6. 4. 11)* tells us that at Leuktra (371) the Lakedaimonian cavalry was extremely poor because horses actually belonged to the richest men in the state. The cavalrymen were only given horses and weapons when the army was mobilised, and they had to take the field at a moment's notice. Furthermore, it was those weakest of body and least loving of glory that served in the cavalry.

So the problem of the state providing sufficient horses for the cavalry was overcome by forcing the richest citizens, perhaps *perioikoi* as well as Spartiates, to contribute their horses upon mobilisation. The manpower for this new formation came from citizens who were least physically suited for service in the ranks of the infantry. An anecdote preserved in Plutarch *(Mor. 210 F, 234 E)* has King Agesilaos, himself lame, upon seeing a lame Lakonian ask for a horse on mobilisation, exclaim: 'Don't you realise that war has need not of those who flee, but of those who stand.' If this anecdote could be relied on as historically valid, it would confirm the testimony of Xenophon.

If we are to believe two anecdotes preserved by Plutarch *(Mor. 234 E, 241 E)*, the manpower shortage became so acute that the lame were also conscripted for infantry service. In the first anecdote a lame man was setting out for war when some people followed him and mocked him. He told them that in war it was only necessary to stand in the rank and not to run away from the enemy. In the second a mother accompanies her lame son as he set out on campaign and says: 'Son, remember your courage with each step.' Clearly the second is a doublet, casting doubt on the accuracy of the first.

Given the inadequacies of their cavalry, the Lakedaimonians started to recruit mercenaries. Xenophon *(Hipparch. 9. 4)* tells us that the fame of the Lakedaimonian cavalry dates to the introduction of mercenaries. Perhaps he is thinking of the recruiting activities of Agesilaos in Asia in 396/5. Agesilaos' first campaigning season in Asia revealed that the army, though superior in infantry, lacked the supporting arms, especially cavalry, to enable them to operate freely in the plains and give them victory over the Persians. Consequently, he assigned to all the richest men in the Asian cities the duty of raising horses. In order that the manpower of the newly raised cavalry force would be of the highest quality, he proclaimed that anyone who supplied a horse and arms and

This 4th century gravestone in the Sparta Museum (565) shows an adolescent male, perhaps the hero Kadmos, being attacked by a snake. In his right hand he defends himself with a knife even smaller than the small Lakonian sword. It may be a Lakonian *xueμιeμ*, or whittling-knife. The limestone stele is so heavily patinated that little detail can be made out. (M.N. Tod & A.J.B. Wace, *Catalogue of the Sparta Museum*, 1906)

Dedication to Castor and Poly-deukes by Menandros, the Lakedaimonian harmost of Kythera, dating to the early 3rd century. Their left hands, resting on their hips, may be holding sword hilts. (National Museum Athens 1437)

a competent substitute cavalryman would not be liable for service himself. Instead of trying to avoid their obligations, the rich who did not want to serve set about looking for substitutes as quickly as possible *(Xen., Hell. 3. 4. 15)*.

On being ordered to return to Europe the following year, Agesilaos was forced to cross hostile Thessaly with his army drawn up in hollow square and threatened by the Thessalian cavalry, then considered to be the best in Greece. Agesilaos managed to outmanoeuvre his adversaries with his own cavalry and force them to break off their pursuit. He then set up a trophy, extremely pleased with his exploit, for he had defeated an enemy which prided itself in its horsemanship with the cavalry he had created himself *(Xen., Ages. 2. 5)*. Mercenary cavalry henceforth remained a feature of the Lakedaimonian army, and in his Boeotian campaign of 377-376 Agesilaos commanded no fewer than 1,500 horsemen *(Diod. 15. 32. 1)*.

The original force of 400 cavalry may have been divided into four *lochoi*. When the army was reorganised into six *morai*, the cavalry was expanded to 600 and divided into six *morai*, each commanded by a *hipparmostes*. Thus the *mora* truly was a 'division', with its own integral cavalry. The cavalry *mora* was divided into two *oulamoi*, each of 50 men drawn up in ten half-files of five. Each of these half-files was called a *pempas*, or 'five', and was commanded by a *pempadarchos*. Two files were known as a *dekas* and commanded by a *dekadarchos*. After the battle of Leuktra the *oulamois* and the *pempas* seem to have been retained, but the *pempas* may have been expanded to six men.

In 392, during the battle of the Long Walls at Corinth, Pasimachos the Lakedaimonian *hipparmostes*, on seeing the Sikyonian infantrymen hard pressed by their Argive opponents, dismounted, together with a few cavalrymen, took the shields from the Sikyonian infantrymen, and fought as infantry to try and stop the rout in the line. In imitation of the Lakedaimonian hoplites, the Sikyonians has painted the initial letter of the name of their city (*sigma*) on their shields. It is said that Pasimachos declared: 'By Castor and Polydeukes, Argives, these *sigmas* will fool you.' Thinking they were only facing Sikyonians, not Lakedaimonians, the Argives advanced without fear and killed Pasimachos and most of his

Broken relief showing a horseman, possibly originally from a tombstone. The relief is not of Attic workmanship. It was found incorporated in a small house on the Athenian Acropolis which was demolished at the beginning of the 20th century and was presumably imported to Athens as ship's ballast in the early modern period. The marble is of a blue-grey type not found in Attica or the Islands but similar to marble used in Lakonia. Thus it may be of Lakonian manufacture. (National Museum Athens)

men. This incident *(Xen., Hell. 4. 4. 10)* shows that Lakedaimonian cavalrymen would not be equipped in a noticeably different manner from either Lakonian or Sikyonian infantry, for otherwise the Argives would have noticed they were not Sikyonian infantry.

Archers

The Lakedaimonians despised archery. The Lakedaimonian way was to fight as heavy infantrymen at close quarters; any other form of warfare was cowardly. Plutarch *(Mor. 234 E)* records the words of a Lakonian as he lay mortally wounded by an arrow. He was not troubled by his imminent death, but that it was at the hands of a 'womanish' archer and before he had accomplished anything.

The Lakedaimonian garrison at Sphakteria surrendered in 425 after enduring the withering archery of their enemy. One of the Athenian allies sneeringly asked a survivor if the dead were the famous 'brave and fair' of the Lakedaimonians, implying that the survivors were neither brave nor fair. Up to that time no Greek had ever imagined that a Lakedaimonian would surrender so long as he had a weapon in his hand. The prisoner replied that it would be 'a fine spindle that could distinguish the brave'. The word spindle *(atrakon)*, which he uses in the place of arrow-shaft, implies that he too considered archery to be 'womanish'.

However, following this surrender, a force of archers of unstated size was raised. We hear nothing further of this force and no archers are mentioned as participating in the battle of Mantineia in 418. The archers may have been raised locally, but they are more likely to have been a mercenary force, perhaps of Cretans, as Sparta had close contacts with several Cretan cities. The army which Cyrus the Younger, a pretender to the Persian throne, assembled with Lakedaimonian support in 401 included a company of 200 Cretan archers, commanded by one Stratokles *(Xen., An. 1. 2. 9, 4. 2. 28)*. A company of 300 Cretan archers is mentioned accompanying the Lakedaimonian army at the Battle of the

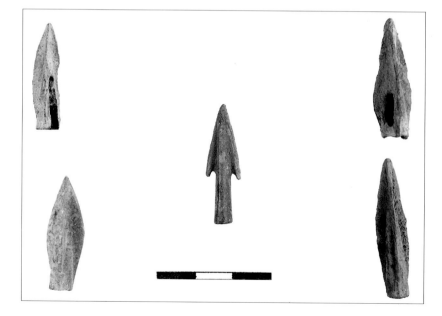

Arrowheads recovered from the sanctuary of Zeus Messapeus at Tsakona, near Sparta. The one in the centre is possibly from the Greek Archaic period, and could attest to an indigenous archery tradition in Lakonia. (British School at Athens 85 [1990] pl. 5b)

Nemea in 394, as well as 400 slingers from the Eleian communities of the Marganeis, Letrinoi and Amphidoloi. The Lakedaimonian reliance on Cretans is further attested in 388: in that year King Agesipolis managed to advance as far as the walls of Argos. The Argives left in the city panicked and shut the gates on the allied Boeotian cavalry. The Boeotians were forced to cling 'like bats' to the walls beneath the battlements. The Lakedaimonians could not reach them with their spears, and had 'the Cretans' not been absent on a raid, many men and horses would have been shot by their arrows *(Xen., Hell. 4. 7. 6)*. A number of sources mention Cretans participating in the Mantineian Campaign of 362, when a Cretan reported to the Spartans that the Theban commander Epaminondas was about to make a surprise attack on their undefended city *(eg. Xen., Hell. 7. 5. 10)*. The companies of archers the Spartan commanders raised in Asia Minor in the early 390s were presumably mercenaries, but we have no clue as to their origins.

Skiritai

Skiritis was a mountainous area of Arcadia, bordering Lakonia. It is clear that the 600 Skiritai who fought at the Battle of Mantineia in 418 were hoplites. In an earlier stage of the same campaign the Lakedaimonians had had an opportunity to see allied Boeotian cavalry and *hamippoi* in operation, perhaps for the first time. *Hamippoi* were light infantry trained to run alongside cavalry and support them. At some point after the battle, the Lakedaimonians either ordered or persuaded the Skiritai to exchange their hoplite equipment for that of *hamippoi*. The Skiritai numbered 600 – the same as the horsemen in the six Lakedaimonian *morai* – so it is possible they were sometimes attached to the cavalry on a one-to-one basis, although we have no proof of this.

A description of the new tactical role of the Skiritai comes in Xenophon's description of a skirmish between Lakedaimonian and Boeotian forces at Tanagra in 377 *(Hell. 5. 4. 52-3)*. The Boeotian infantry were stationed at the top of a hill, but a feint by Agesilaos convinced them that he was making for the undefended city of Thebes. They began to retire from the hill at a run, and the Skiritai and some of the cavalry climbed the hill and began to shower blows upon the hindmost Thebans. In the event, the Skiritai pursued too closely, for as soon as the Thebans neared the gates of the city, they turned round and stood fast, upon which the Skiritai fell back, in Xenophon's ironic words, 'at a faster pace than a walk'.

Xenophon *(Cyr. 4. 2. 1)* tells us that the Lakedaimonians spared the Skiritai 'neither in hardships nor in danger'. Together with the cavalry scouts, the Skiritai were employed to scout ahead of the main body on the march and to patrol outside the camp lines at night *(Lac. Pol. 12. 3, 13. 6)*.

Peltasts

As Skiritis was an allied community, not an integral part of Lakedaimon, the Skiritai only fought alongside the Lakedaimonian cavalry when the allies were mobilised for a major campaign. In other circumstances the Lakedaimonian cavalry had to rely upon the close support of peltasts. These companies of peltasts seem to have been mercenaries. This does not rule out their being native Lakonians, but it makes it highly unlikely.

In the 379 expedition of Cleombrotus to Boeotia the peltasts were deployed in front of the army *(Xen., Hell. 5. 4. 14)*. In the following year Agesilaos made another expedition to Boeotia with an army which included mercenary peltasts who operated with units of cavalry. The latter included Theban exiles as well as Spartiates and *perioikoi*. When the citizen army withdrew from Boeotia, Agesilaos left the peltasts behind in Thespiai as a garrison, under the command of the harmost Phoibidas. When the Thebans invaded Thespian territory, Phoibidas had great success with his peltasts, harrying the Theban hoplites and not allowing them to disperse to gather booty. They pushed their advantage too closely, however, for they pursued the Theban cavalry as far as an impassable ravine, forcing the Thebans to make a desperate counter-attack in which the peltasts were routed and Phoibidas killed *(Xen., Hell.*

Fragment of an Athenian relief honouring the dead lost in a year of the late 5th or early 4th century. The fallen hoplite is Athenian. The figure running behind is dressed in an *exomis* tunic and a *pilos* cap. He uses an animal skin wrapped around his left shoulder as both a cloak and a shield. Note the left hand is clasped, as if holding a spear shaft, which would have been painted in the relief in its original state. He may hold a short sword in his left hand. He is equipped in a manner suitable for a *hamippos*, and therefore could be a Skiritan. (New York, Metropolitan Museum, Fletcher Fund, 1929)

5. 4. 39-45). The 'mercenaries under Hieron' who accompanied the Phocian peltasts and the cavalry of the Herakleiots and Phliasians in the initial attack upon the Boeotian army at the battle of Leuctra in 371, were presumably peltasts too; perhaps even the same regiment under a new commander (*Xen., Hell. 6. 4. 9*).

Skiritis became independent after the battle of Leuctra, in 371, and the Lakedaimonians had to rely exclusively on their companies of peltasts to perform the tasks previously carried out by the Skiritai. For example, Xenophon (*Lac. Pol. 12. 3*) tells us that the duty of patrolling outside the camp lines once performed by the Skiritai became the duty of "the mercenaries", presumably peltasts. In 365, in the operation to relieve the Lakedaimonian garrison at Kromnos, the peltasts are described as running on ahead of the king, Archidamus (*Xen., Hell. 7. 4. 22*). We learn of various forces of mercenaries during the period after Leuctra. Their troop-type is not stated, but they could have been either hoplites or peltasts. We also learn of a unit of mercenaries stationed in the Arcadian town of Orchomenos during the 370 invasion of Lakonia, and in the following year Philiskos, an envoy of the Persian king Artaxerxes II, left 2,000 selected mercenaries with the Lakedaimonians. The mercenary force which Xenophon mentions as being absent in Arcadia when the Thebans launched their surprise attack on Sparta, in 362 (*Xen., Hell. 7. 5. 10*), may well have included units of peltasts as well as the Cretan archers.

CONCLUSION

We have seen the Lakedaimonians emerge from these pages as an innovating force in ancient Greek warfare. The organisation of the army was kept up to date by periodic reforms, and the arms carried were of the latest design. The Lakedaimonians were at the forefront of tactical developments and may indeed have been the initiators of many of them. Perhaps the most important of these was the part Lakedaimonian military theorists played in the evolution of the divisional concept – a division being defined as a formation 'which combines in itself the necessary arms and services required for sustained combat'. As far as European warfare is concerned, the creation of the *mora* (the word itself means 'division') is the first recorded example of an army being separated into divisions which each contained both cavalry and infantry and was each capable of independent operations. This professional and intellectual approach to warfare put Sparta at the head of Greece for two centuries. It lost this dominant position at Leuktra in 371 not through lack of military skill, but as a result of its growing manpower crisis. According to Aristotle, 'a single blow was too much for the city, ruined by its sparsity of population" (*Politics 2. 6. 8*) .

THE PLATES

A: WARRIORS IN THE AGE OF LYCURGUS

This plate shows the appearance of three Spartan warriors in the last decades of the 8th century, when Helos was enslaved and Spartan power reached the mouth of the Eurotas. At this time the hoplite shield had not been developed and hoplite tactics had not been introduced.

Figure A1 wears a Corinthian helmet of the earliest type. His bell cuirass is based on the earliest example known, from a Late Geometric warrior grave in Argos which dates to c.725. He holds his Dipylon shield by its central handle, together with a spare spear. Most warriors in Homer carry a pair of dual-purpose spears which can be used either as javelins or for close-quarter fighting. The Dipylon shield may have been made of wicker and leather rather than wood, and is reconstructed as such. Shields of this type are named after the Dipylon Gate in Athens, where pottery decorated with these 'incuse' shields was discovered by early excavators. All three figures have very early 'prototype' versions of the traditional hoplite greave, barely covering the length of the shin and as yet with no attempt to show the musculature.

Figure A2 carries his Dipylon shield slung over his back with a strap called the *telamoµn*. He wears a helmet of the type known as a 'Kegelhelm', where neck- and cheek-pieces are riveted to a conical cap. Unlike the other two warriors, he carries a single large fighting spear, tipped by a large spearhead (of Snodgrass Type E3) about 40cm long. He also carries a 'Naue II' type sword, and his abdomen is protected by a bronze belt.

As well as various types of non-metallic shield, occasional examples of bronze-faced 'Herzsprung' shields have been found at shrines such as Delphi or Idalion in Cyprus. Named after a find-spot in Northern Germany, these shields are most commonly found in Central Europe. The V-shaped notch in the centre probably reflects the original leather construction of this type of shield.

Figure A3 carries a Herzsprung shield which he has stripped

Fragment of a 7th century bronze warrior's belt. It is decorated with a scene of fighting warriors with Dipylon shields. From the sanctuary known as the Menelaion, near Sparta. (Lakonikai Spoudai 8, [1986] 46-7)

from the body of a fallen enemy. The shield may have been produced outside Greece. Armour was tremendously expensive and many warriors must have re-used captured weapons. His bronze helmet is of an open-faced type.

B: THE SECOND MESSENIAN WAR

This plate is based on a battle scene on a Late Protocorinthian vase, once in the Chigi collection, showing a piper. Some have suggested that the use of pipers was once quite general. However, only the Spartan army is definitely known to have used pipers, and so it is possible that the artist included the piper deliberately as a sign that it was the Spartan army he was showing. We could be dealing with one of the earliest representations of Spartan hoplites in colour. Some 26cm high, the vase is decorated in four horizontal friezes, painted in a miniaturist style. The topmost frieze shows a battle scene: one of the earliest undisputed depictions of a hoplite battle. Photography is difficult, given the size and shape of the vase, so readers are directed to the excellent colour reconstruction of the battle scene in Peter Connolly's *Greece and Rome at War* (1981). The vase dates to the years 650-625 and could conceivably represent a battle during the Second Messenian War, which broke out in the 660s and lasted many years.

The rim of the hoplite shield was covered by a bronze strip, decorated with the almost inevitable guilloche (cable) pattern. The uppermost leather layer of the main body of the shield was painted, as was the rim. The base colour is yellow, perhaps imitating bronze. The left arm is passed through a bronze arm-band (*porpax*) as far as the elbow, and the left hand grasps a handle (*antilabe*) secured to the rim. On these shields it seems that the forearm and shoulder are protected by extra reinforcing layers of leather glued to the inside of the shield. These reinforcements were later made of bronze. The significance of the shield-blazons used by the opponents of the Spartan line, if they have any, is not known. Of the four Spartan warriors shown in full at the front of the scene, two wear no tunic under their corselet, while the other two wear crimson tunics, and so it is possible that the crimson tunic had become standard in the Spartan army even by this early date. The warriors carry two spears, not one, and throwing thongs can be seen on some of the spears. Furthermore, none of the spears has the bronze butt-spike (*sauroter*) of the later hoplite spear. Thus the transition from 'Homeric' warfare, when the spear had a dual function, is not yet complete. It may be significant that Tyrtaios *(frg. 8. 30 F)*, who lived at the time of the Second Messenian War, mentions javelins being thrown from under the cover of shields. Swords are not shown on the vase.

C: THE SPARTAN KINGS, EARLY 6TH CENTURY

A terracotta plaque from Sparta shows two warriors whose helmets are decorated with transverse crests. In later Greek military practice, rank can be represented by the type of crest, and so it is just possible that these two warriors are meant to represent the two kings of Sparta. The colours of the inside and outside of the shields of the two kings **(Figures C1, C2)** are based on a miniature terracotta shield from Sparta. At this time, shields seem to be predominately decorated with geometric patterns. Behind the kings can be seen the standard of Sparta. The *dokana*, or 'beam-figures', were a symbolic representation of the brotherly love of Castor and Polydeukes, the military protectors of Sparta, and were carried in front of the army on campaign.

Figure C3 is based on a Lakonian warrior statuette from

Miniature terracotta shield found at Sparta. The inside is decorated with an incised scale-pattern in red, black and white. The outside is decorated in radial crescents in red, black and white, and outside that by a red band; beyond that the rim is black and decorated with white dots with red centres. (British School at Athens 29 [1927-28] 100)

Olympia, which is included in this plate because of the interest of its non-standard helmet, made up of a number of plates. The cheek-piece is scalloped, leaving an aperture for the mouth. Cheek-pieces of this type are also shown on other Lakonian representational evidence, and, more importantly, an actual cheek-piece of this type has been recovered from Sparta. This statuette now confirms that helmets such as this type continued to be used well into the 6th century. The shield pattern is based on those of contemporary miniature lead figurines from the shrine of Artemis Orthia.

D: SPARTAN WARRIORS C.530 BC

The three figures are shown inside an ancient temple in Sparta. The first two figures show the attempts made by the Spartans and other Greeks c.550-525 to augment the protection afforded by the hoplite panoply. **Figure D1** is based on the warrior statuette from Longa. He wears extra items to protect his thighs and right arm, as well as the standard elements of the hoplite panoply. Note the heavy relief patterns decorating the cuirass. **Figure D2,** based on a Lakonian warrior statuette from Dodona, wears a helmet of the Illyrian type, so-named because a large number of early finds came from Illyria. However, it is now clear that it was also extremely popular in the Peloponnese, which is the most probable area of origin. The bell cuirass is in its final stage of development and the groin is protected by eight groin-flaps. They are presumably bronze and may have been attached to a belt worn under the cuirass. Not all hoplites took advantage of the new protective armour, as is shown by **Figure D3,** based on a Lakonian warrior statuette now in the National Museum, Athens. Note the six locks combed straight back under the helmet. The shield device is based on a bronze shield-blazon from Sparta.

E: THE BATTLE OF THERMOPYLAE, 480 BC

If the Persian Wars were the most glorious period in Spartan history, then the battle of Thermopylae was surely Sparta's finest hour. The Spartans used an apparently novel tactic: they pretended to run away, and then turned to defeat their disorganised enemy pursuers *(Hdt. 7. 211)*. Such a tactic would only work when carried out by highly trained troops.

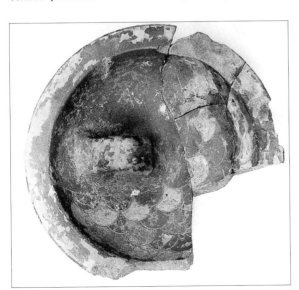

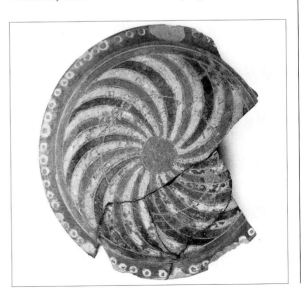

When news came that the paths through the Kallidromos Mountains were betrayed to the Persians, King Leonidas knew that his force was in danger of being cut off. Therefore he dismissed the Greek forces, keeping with him only his own force of 300 Spartans, the Theban contingent of 400 (effectively hostages) which he expected to go over to the Persians, and the Thespian contingent of 700 men, who refused to leave Leonidas' side, commanded by Demophilus, son of Diadromes.

The Greeks inflicted heavy casualties in the first phase of the final battle, killing two brothers of Xerxes. Leonidas too lost his life. His body was recovered after a desperate fight, and the Greeks withdrew to a small hill at the entrance to the pass, to make a final stand. By this stage many had had their spears broken in their hands. Others had lost their swords and had to fight on with their hands and teeth. The Persians decided to kill them by missiles alone, so as not to lose further men. It is said that the Spartan Dienekes was the bravest man who took part in the battle. Before the battle someone had remarked that when the Persians shot their arrows, the sun was blotted out by their number. He replied that this was indeed good news, as they would now fight in the shade. After him, the bravest Spartans were the brothers Alpheos and Maron, sons of Orsiphantos, and the bravest Thespian was Dithyrambos, son of Harmatides. The following epitaph, which was put over the tomb of the Spartans, became legendary:

Oh stranger, tell the Lakedaimonians that here
we lie, obedient to their commands

A Lakonian bronze warrior statuette from Dodona preserves the appearance of a Spartan hoplite during the Persian Wars. All the warriors in Plate D are based on this figure. The cuirass is one of the latest examples of the bell type, and so is quite old-fashioned for the period. Once again, the long hair is to be noted. Xerxes is said to have been surprised when his spies reported that the Spartans were exercising and combing their hair before the battle *(Hdt. 7. 208)*. We have no clues as to the appearance of the Thespian hoplites.

The degree to which the Lakedaimonian army had become uniform in its dress and equipment by the

Persian Wars is not known. There would have been a certain amount of standardisation in equipment, simply because the bell cuirasses and Corinthian helmets in use at this time were almost identical, thought slight differences would have existed. The plume on the Corinthian helmet of the Dodona statuette is raised, whereas most other statuettes have plumes flush with the helmet. Minor variations in details of dress, such as tunic decoration, may also be expected.

F: AMOMPHARETOS AT THE BATTLE OF PLATAEA, 479 BC

Having failed to hold the pass at Thermopylae, the Greek armies retreated into the Peloponnese. Following a decisive defeat of the Persian fleet at Salamis, Xerxes retreated to Asia with the majority of the Persian army. This enabled the Greeks to advance into Boeotia the following year, where they encamped on the Plain of Asopus. The Greek army retreated from its exposed position on the plain after suffering casualties from the Persian archers and after the Persians had choked up the spring at Gargaphia, from which the Greek forces were drawing their water. After nightfall the various contingents of the army started their withdrawal except for the Lakedaimonians. Amompharetos, the *lochagos* of the Pitanate *lochos*, refused to retreat in the face of the enemy and thus disgrace Sparta. His blind obedience to Spartan precepts of military honour threatened the division of the Greek forces and their destruction piecemeal. The regent (called *prodikos* by the Lakedaimonians) Pausanias, who commanded the Lakedaimonian army, and his kinsman Euryanax attempted to persuade Amompharetos to lead his *lochos* to the rear, threatening to leave them to die. At this moment an Athenian herald approached, sent by the Athenians to find out what was happening. He witnessed the

Fragment of a moulded clay relief from Sparta. The excavator Woodward suggested that the crests are shown transversely to avoid 'the difficulty of showing the crest from the front'. (British School at Athens 29, 1927-28)

culmination of the argument. The Greeks used to vote using small pebbles as their ballots. Amompharetos picked up a huge rock with both hands and threw it down at Pausanias' feet, shouting: 'There is my vote against fleeing before the foreigners!' *(Hdt. 9. 55)*. Daybreak found the army in its same position, and it was only then that Pausanias began his retreat without the Pitanate *lochos*. Amompharetos reluctantly followed. The untidy retreat of the Greeks encouraged the Persians to pursue them incautiously, which, in turn, brought about the Persian defeat.

To the right stands the Athenian herald **(Figure F1)**. Heralds were distinguished by the sceptres they carried, and a number are shown on Greek vase-paintings. To the left of the figures of Pausanias **(Figure F2)** and behind him Euryanax **(Figure F3)** are based on the Wadsworth Athenaeum statuette. In the centre is Amompharetos **(Figure F4)**, based on the Dodona statuette like the warriors in Plate E. As a senior officer, he may have worn a transverse crest on his helmet, like that of Pausanias. The Spartan soldiers looking on in the background have shield devices based on those shown on contemporary lead figurines of warriors from the shrine of Artemis Orthia.

G: SPARTAN ARMY, C.470 BC

This plate represents a scene behind the battle-line of the Lakedaimonian army during the difficult period c.475-450, when the state had to fight for its survival against a combination of a major revolt of the Messenian helots and alliances of enemies. **Figure G1** is sacrificing a female goat to Artemis Agrotera, before the final advance towards the enemy line. The lack of relevant archaeological material for this period means that any reconstruction of the appearance of a warrior remains highly speculative. However, it seems reasonable to

assume that the Corinthian helmet remained in use well into the 5th century, before being replaced by the pilos-helmet. It also seems reasonable to assume that the bell cuirass was replaced by a 'muscle' cuirass of the normal Greek type for the period, either with or without hinged shoulder-pieces. Greaves may also have continued in use for some time. Behind him stand a piper and a trumpeter **(Figures G2, G3)**. It is not known whether the trumpeters, heralds and pipers of the army would be dressed in crimson like the combatants. Presumably so, although the piper on the Chigi vase is dressed in black. It is possible that the latter colour had some significance, assuming that the Lakedaimonian army is, in fact, shown on this vase.

H: THE FIRST BATTLE OF MANTINEIA, 418 BC

In this plate we see soldiers resting after the First Battle of Mantineia. **Figure H1** represents a Lakedaimonian hoplite of the period and is based on the vase decorated by *'The Painter of the Berlin Dancing Girl'*, so called after a vase in Berlin showing a dancing girl, with the addition of a crimson *exomis* tunic. He takes a drink from his drinking-mug (*kothon*). Behind him, **Figure H2** represents a junior officer, with his pilos-helmet decorated with a plume. The shape of the plume is based on a figure from Sparta. It is not known whether all soldiers wore a plume on their pilos-helmets on special occasions such as parades and perhaps battles, or whether they were used as a badge of rank. Though no Lakonian examples have survived, there are representations of pilos-helmets with transverse plumes. These could be interpreted as distinctive plumes worn by senior commanders. Thus **Figure H3** represents a Lakedaimonian senior commander.

On the ground lies a dead Mantineian's shield. A fragment

In legend, Castor and Polydeukes were twin sons of King Tyndareus of Lakedaimon so are called the 'Tyndaridai' or 'Sons of Tyndareus'. According to another version, they were twin sons of Zeus, and so can also be called the 'Dioskouroi' or 'Sons of Zeus'. The most important centre of their cult was Lakedaimon, where they were symbolised by the *dokana*, two upright pieces of wood connected by two cross-beams, shown on this gravestone from Sparta. (M.N. Tod & A.J.B. Wace, *Catalogue of the Sparta Museum*, 1906)

from a poem by Bacchylides runs: 'How the Mantineians bear the trident on their shields wrought of bronze'. The trident was the symbol of Poseidon, the patron god of Mantineia. The context of the poem would seem to be a list of Greek forces present at some battle. The year of Bacchylides' death is not known, but we do know that his last dated poem was written in 452, and it is unlikely that he lived much longer. So this is the first literary reference to a state symbol used as a shield device, probably c.475-450. The shape of the trident copies that shown on 5th and 4th century coins of Mantineia.

I: LYSANDER'S FLEET AT AIGOSPOTAMOI, 405 BC

According to Lakedaimonian law, the post of admiral (navarchos) could not be held for more than one year at a time. For this reason, at Aigospotamoi the talented com-

mander Lysander was serving as the notional secretary (epistoleus) to the admiral Arakos.

We are only patchily informed about the composition of the fleet. It was mainly an allied one, with ships initially paid for and commanded by captains (trierarchai) from the allied cities. The rowers used by all fleets during this campaign seem to have been hired, as were the steersmen **(Figure I 1)** and other senior skilled sailors of the crew. The steersman of Lysander's own ship was a Megarian named Hermon. For most of the campaign, in fact, the fleet was sustained by Persian money.

As well as its crew, each ship had a complement of marines. **Figure I 2** represents an allied hoplite marine. His shield device may have been used by some of the Asiatic allied contingents, since it is a common device on the coins of various member cities in the alliance. The rowers would almost certainly have been naked, so too probably the marines, since they might have had to swim if the ship sank. We do not know if the ships of Lysander's fleet were also given archers. The Corinthians, at least, possessed a corps of archers which may have been used on their ships. **Figure I 3** represents a naval archer. Presumably they would not have worn armour in case they were forced to swim.

J: THE *WORKSHOP OF WAR*, EPHESOS 396-395 BC

The Persian war increased in tempo in 396, when King Agesilaos was sent out with an expeditionary force of 2,000 neodamodeis and a contingent of 6,000 allies, with 30

LEFT **Lakonian bronze figurine from the temple of Apollo Korythos in Messenia (modern Longa). As well as the armguards and thigh-guards, we might see him wearing ankle- and foot- guards, if the feet were not broken off the statuette. (Athens, National Museum 14789)**

BELOW **Shield devices shown on miniature lead figurines that were found in their thousands at the shrine of Artemis Orthia in Sparta. More naturalistic devices were to come in during the 6th century. (R.M. Dawkins, *Artemis Orthia*, 1929)**

Spartiates serving as staff-officers and formation and unit commanders *(Xen., Hell. 3. 4. 3)*.

Figure J1 represents a Lakedaimonian senior officer. *Perioikoi* (citizens of Lakedaimonian cities other than Sparta) and sometimes even helots it seems, held senior commands abroad as well as Spartiates. This officer wears all the dress which distinguished a Lakedaimonian abroad: a Lakonian *pilos* cap, a thin crimson *tribon* wrapped tightly around the body, red Lakonian sandals and a Lakonian staff. When the *tribon* was worn, the shoulder-high staff could be tucked under the armpit to hold the folds of the cloak firmly in place and so leave the arms free.

Figure J2 attempts a reconstruction of one of Agesilaos' regiments of Ionian mercenary cavalry. A fragment of Demokritos of Ephesos preserved in Athenaeus *(12. 525 C-E)* tells us that the garments of the Ionians were dyed violet and woven with diamonds of crimson and yellow, and had upper borders decorated with evenly-spaced animal patterns. Athenian vase paintings of the 400s and 390s by the Suessula painter and others, show tunics which seem to be of this Ionian type. This figure of an Ionian cavalryman is based on the Lakedaimonian heroes Castor and Polydeukes, as shown on such vases.

In the winter of 396-395 the whole army was gathered at Ephesos. Agesilaos organised competitions and offered prizes for the fittest hoplite unit and the cavalry unit most skilled in horsemanship. Similar prizes were offered to the units of peltasts and archers. Immediately the gymnasia filled with athletes and the hippodrome with cavalrymen, and archers and peltasts could be seen practising everywhere. 'The marketplace was crowded with horses and arms of all kinds for sale, and the braziers, carpenters, smiths, curriers and painters were all engaged in preparing equipment for the field; so that a person might really have thought the city to be a workshop of war.'*(Xen., Hell. 3. 4. 17)*

Figure J3 represents an Ephesian painter, clothed in a mixture of Greek and Persian dress which may have been common in the city. Plutarch *(Vit. Lys. 3. 2)* claims that when Lysander made Ephesos his base during the Peloponnesian War, although the Ephesians welcomed him, they were in danger of becoming thoroughly barbarised by the admixture of Persian customs, since the city was surrounded on all sides by Lydia, and was the Persian naval headquarters in the Aegean. Demokritos of Ephesos tells us that, among their other luxuries, the Ephesians wore Persian tunics (*sarapeis*) of quince yellow, crimson, white and even purple. They also wore long Persian robes similar to the Egyptian *kalasiris*, which were the finest of all. One might also see, continues Demokritos, the so-called *aktaiai*, the most costly of all Persian robes, covered all over in gold beads. The painter is seen decorating a shield with the bee symbol of Ephesos, suitable for the Ephesian contingent of hoplites of the allied phalanx. After Lysander's fall from power, the *Herakliskos Drakopnignon* ceases to be the common coin device, so would hardly have been used as a common shield device. Therefore the use of individual city shield-blazons may have been resumed.

The Asian cities of the alliance were apparently organised

LEFT **Lakonian warrior statuette found at Dodona in 1930. The Corinthian helmet is shown as very open-faced – too much so for this period. This is presumably a deliberate distortion on the part of the artist. Note the hem of the close-fitting tunic, ornately decorated in a wave-pattern. The warrior seems to have folded his tunic over in the front before putting on his cuirass. (Ioannina Museum)**

RIGHT **Stele from ancient Areopolis, dating to the first half of the 5th century, showing a young *perioikos* warrior. He takes off his armour: first his helmet then his shield. He seems to be wearing a cap-comforter under his helmet, greaves and possibly a muscle-cuirass. The significance of the snake – a symbol of the underworld, immortality and also the attribute of a hero – is not clearly understood. (Athenische Mitteilungen 29, 1904)**

into a number of recruitment districts, which were possibly also tribute districts, imitating the organisation of the Athenian empire it replaced. Xenophon tells us that in the stand-off battle which took place in the Plain of the Maeander in 397 the allied phalanx was divided into *taxeis* and *lochoi*. Presumably each city supplied a *lochos* to the *taxis* of its recruiting district. During the battle 'the men from Priene and Achilleion, from the Islands and from the Ionian cities' ran way from the battle-line *(Xen., Hell. 3. 2. 17)*. The men of Priene in Ionia and Achilleion on the Hellespont are probably specifically mentioned because they were the first to turn tail: these would be *lochoi*. The Islanders and Ionians would be *taxeis*. At the battle of Koroneia in 395, Xenophon *(Ages. 2. 11)* mentions formations of Ionians, Aeolians and Hellespontines within the allied phalanx, presumably *taxeis*.

K: MERCENARY INFANTRY REGIMENTS, 396-395 BC

The other hoplite formations of Agesilaos' army would have been distinguished by their shield blazons. The force of 2,000 *neodamodeis* presumably decorated their shields with the letter *lambda*, as did all Lakedaimonian formations. Similarly, the European allies who accompanied the expedition would probably have used their own state shield blazons.

One pre-existing formation of mercenaries which the Lakedaimonians had incorporated into their army was the remains of the 10,000 Greek mercenaries who accompanied Cyrus the Younger in his campaign of 401. These troops were placed under the command of the Spartan Herripidas, but they retained their title of 'Kyreioi', or 'Cyreans'. In 401 the Kyreioi had all worn helmets (presumably pilos-helmets) of bronze, crimson tunics and greaves *(Xen., An. 1. 2. 16)*. It is possible that they may have decorated their shields with a crimson letter *kappa* in order to proclaim their regimental title. **Figure K1** attempts a reconstruction of their appearance.

We hear of a second formation of mercenaries in the service of Agesilaos. These were raised by an earlier Spartan general called Derkylidas. Their title, *Derkylideioi*, is preserved in a single passage in a fragmented papyrus source known as the *Hellenica Oxyrhynchia (21[16]. 2)*. In 399 Derkylidas campaigned in the Troad, where he liberated many of the cities from the rule of the local sub-satrap, Meidias the Dardanian. He incorporated Meidias' mercenary forces into the Lakedaimonian army *(Xen., Hell.*

Terracotta votive plaque, probably dating to *c*.450-425, from the shrine of Alexandra/Kassandra and Agamemnon at Amyklai, now in the Sparta Museum (6225/1). Note the Corinthian helmet worn pushed back and the rather short leaf-shaped sword. Faint traces of red paint have been preserved on the crest and grey paint on the sword-blade. (Hesperia 66, 1997)

3. 1. 23). It is presumably these troops who were called 'Derkylideians', a title which, like the Kyreioi, they retained after the death of thier namesake. They may have been distinguished by a Greek letter *delta* painted on their shields, as in **Figure K2**.

The level of speculation in the previous two reconstructions must be admitted, but we do know that a large degree of uniformity in dress existed among the units of Agesilaos' army. Upon his recall to Europe, Agesilaos left a garrison of 4,000 men behind, but in order to maintain morale in the rest of the force destined to return to Europe, he held another series of competitions, with prizes for the best hoplite *lochos* from the Asian cities, the best mercenary *lochos* of hoplites, archers and peltasts, and the best force of cavalry *(Hell. 4. 2. 5)*. This passage, incidentally, informs us that the archers and peltasts in the army were mercenaries. The prizes included sets of weapons. Agesilaos' army met the enemies of Sparta at the battle of Chaironeia, where, so armed, it appeared as 'a mass of bronze and crimson' *(Ages. 2. 7)*. The King, said Xenophon 'prided himself on the simplicity of his own dress and the splendid equipment of his army' *(Ages. 11. 11)*.

We know much less about the non-hoplite components of Agesilaos' army. In 399 Seuthes, prince of the Thracian tribe of the Odrysians, had sent a force of 200 horsemen and 300 peltasts to help the Lakedaimonians *(Xen., Hell. 3. 2. 2)*. From time to time the army also included other non-Greek units. However, the majority of the units of archers, peltasts and cavalrymen in the army were presumably Greeks. Some may have been existing mercenary units taken into Lakedaimonian service, while other units may have been newly formed locally. **Figure K3** is heavily armoured with a composite cuirass. It may be that some units of archers, unable to use a shield for protection at the same time as they used their bow, were armoured, to afford some protection from enemy missiles. Such troops would be especially useful in sieges, such as that shown on the Nereid Monument.

L: A SKIRMISH NEAR TANAGRA, 377 BC

A Lakedaimonian cavalryman of the late 5th and 4th centuries (**Figure L1**) probably resembled the horse-riding national heroes Castor and Polydeukes, who are often depicted on reliefs of this date. The heroes are shown wearing Lakonian *piloi* or bronze pilos-helmets. They also wear *exoµmis* tunics, open at the right arm and shoulder and gathered up at the waist in a sort of roll. The reliefs do not show the heroes wearing the *chlamys* cloaks normally seen on a Greek cavalrymen. Instead, they appear to wear the Lakedaimonian *triboµn* type of cloak, wrapped round the body in such a way as to leave the arms free. They carry long spears and swords.

Horse-riding required boots or shoes. In present-day equitation, the boot is placed in the stirrup in such a way as to put pressure on the horse with the thighs. In bareback riding, however, there is much more reliance on the lower leg, which is used to secure the rider's seat and to control the horse.

ABOVE **A pair of archers shown on the Nereid monument of Xanthos. This monument was erected to commemorate the exploits of one of the Lycian dynasts of Xanthos. Its date, and therefore the historical scenes depicted on it, cannot be established with any certainty, though it probably dates to the final decades of the 5th century. As well as hoplites and a number of archers in Asiatic dress, the monument shows these two Greek archers covering the escalade of a city, members of a mercenary company of archers in employment in Asia. (British Museum)**

LEFT **A 4th century bronze statuette, probably showing a warrior taking part in a religious parade. Possibly an ephebe, he is naked and clean-shaven. The crest on his helmet may be a badge of rank, or could have just been worn for the parade. Originally he would have carried a spear and a shield. (Sparta Museum)**

Boots were worn to avoid unpleasant rubbing from the coarse hairy coat of the horse. None of the Castor and Polydeukes reliefs show the boots clearly, so we have restored the open-toed Lakonian sandals, though perhaps a higher version was used by the cavalry.

The Skiritan (**Figure L2**) is based on an Attic relief, possibly showing a soldier of this type. Xenophon *(Hell. 7. 5. 20)* tells us that before the second battle of Mantineia, in 362, the Arcadian hoplites painted clubs on their shields, in imitation of their allies, the Thebans. This was done in order to avoid confusion in the battle. The club was a symbol of Herakles, the patron god of Thebes. Most legends claimed that Herakles was born in Argos or Tiryns, but the Thebans claimed that their city was his birthplace. It is difficult to know how long the club shield-device was in use, but it is shown on late 5th century vases. This Theban hoplite (**Figure L3**) wears an early version of the Boeotian helmet, which was probably adopted by the infantry in the 4th century.

The motif of 'Young Herakles the Snake-Strangler' together with the letters SYN (standing for 'alliance') appears on the coins of Byzantium, Cyzicus, Lampsacus, Ephesos, Samos, Iasus, Cnidus and Rhodes. Stefan Karweise (*Numismatic Chronicle* [1980] 1-27) has demonstrated that these coins were struck during the years 405-400 and commemorate the alliance with Sparta. Herakles, one of whose feats of strength was to strangle snakes as a baby, was an ancestor of Lysander. Here, Herakles represents Lysander and the snakes, the Athenian Empire. (Hirmer Fotoarchiv)

FURTHER READING

A large number of academic books and articles have been published on ancient Sparta including some dealing with military aspects. The views advanced here summarise those which will be advanced in my forthcoming book, *The Spartan Army*, to be published by Oficyna Naukowa MS, PO Box 126, 90-965 Lodz, Poland. The subject is quite contentious however, particularly with regard to army organisation.

J.F. Lazenby, *The Spartan Army* (1985)
This offers a completely different view on the above.

J.K. Anderson, *Military Theory and Practice in the Age of Xenophon* (1970)
Developments in Spartan equipment and tactics in the Classical period.

P. Cartledge, *Hoplites and heroes: Sparta's Contribution to the Technique of Ancient Warfare, Journal of Hellenic Studies 97*, 11-27 (1977)
With regard to evidence for the Archaic period, this makes a number of extremely useful points, some of which have been incorporated in the text above.

Key classical authors consulted include; Plutarch *(Plut.)*, Athenaeus *(Athen.)*, Xenophon *(Xen.)*, Herodotus *(Holt.)*, Thucydides *(Thuc.)*, Lycurgus *(Lycurg.)*, Pausanias *(Paus.)* and Diodorus *(Diod.)*.

RIGHT **Lakonian bronze statuette of a warrior from Olympia. Note the unusual cheek-pieces of the open-faced helmet. (© German Archaeological Institute, Athens)**

LES PLANCHES

A: Guerriers à l'époque de Lycurgus Cette planche dépeint l'apparence de trois guerriers spartiates pendant les dernières décennies du VIIIe siècle, lorqu'Helos fut réduit en esclavage et alors que le pouvoir de Sparte s'étendait jusqu'à l'embouchure de l'Eurotas. A cette époque, le bouclier hoplite n'avait pas encore été inventé et les tactiques hoplites n'avaient pas encore été introduites. Ces trois personnages portent des versions "prototypes" de la cnémide hoplite traditionnelle, qui couvre à peine la longueur du tibia et qui ne présente encore aucune tentative pour mettre la musculature en valeur.

B: La seconde guerre messénienne Cette planche s'inspire d'une scène de bataille décrite sur un vase de la fin de la période proto-corinthienne, qui se trouvait dans la collection Chigi et qui dépeint un joueur de pipeau. Certains ont suggéré que les joueurs de pipeau étaient autrefois assez répandus, mais c'est seulement dans le cas de l'armée spartiate que nous savons avec certitude que des joueurs de pipeau étaient utilisés. Il est donc possible que l'artiste ait inclus ce musicien dans un geste délibéré, pour indiquer que l'armée qu'il dépeignait était celle des Spartiates. Nous avons peut-être ici affaire à l'une des premières représentations des hoplites spartiates en couleur.

C: Les rois spartiates, début du VIe siècle Une plaque en terre cuite de Sparte dépeint deux guerriers dont le casque est décoré de cimiers transversaux. Dans les habitudes militaires grecques plus tardives, le rang est parfois représenté par le type de cimier. Il est donc possible que ces deux guerriers représentent les deux rois de Sparte. Les couleurs de l'intérieur et de l'extérieur du bouclier des deux rois (C1, C2) sont basées sur un bouclier miniature en terre cuite de Sparte. C3 est basé sur la statuette d'un guerrier de Lakonie retrouvée à Olympe, nous l'avons inclus ici à cause de son casque hors normes intéressant, composé de plusieurs plaques.

D: Guerriers spartiates, vers 530 av. J.-C. Le personnage D1 est basé sur la statuette d'un guerrier retrouvé à Longa. D2, basé sur la statuette d'un guerrier retrouvé à Dodona, porte un casque de type Illyrien, ainsi nommé car c'est durant les premières fouilles archéologiques en Illyrie que de nombreux objets furent mis à jour. Certains hoplites n'adoptèrent pas la nouvelle armure protectrice, comme l'indique la figure D3, basée sur la statuette d'un guerrier de Lakonie se trouve aujourd'hui au Musée National d'Athènes.

E: La bataille des Thermopyles, 480 av. J.-C. Si les guerres perses furent la période la plus glorieuse de l'histoire spartiate, la bataille des Thermopyles fut certainement la plus grande heure de Sparte. Les Grecs infligèrent de grosses pertes pendant la première phase de la dernière bataille et tuèrent deux frères de Xerxès. Léonidas succomba lui aussi. Son corps fut regagné après un combat désespéré et les Grecs se retirèrent sur une petite colline à l'entrée du défilé pour opposer une dernière résistance. Beaucoup n'avaient plus qu'une lance brisée, alors que d'autres avaient perdu leur épée et étaient forcés de se battre à mains nues et avec leurs dents. Les Perses décidèrent de les tuer uniquement au moyen de missiles afin de ne pas augmenter leurs pertes.

F: Amompharetos à la bataille de Platée, 479 av. J.-C. Sur la droite, se tient le héraut athénien (F1). Les hérauts étaient reconnaissables grâce au sceptre qu'ils portaient. Sur la gauche, les personnages de Pausanias (F2) et derrière lui Auryanax (F3) sont basés sur la statuette de Wadsworth Athenaeum. Au centre, Amompharetos (F4), basé sur la statuette de Dodona. Les soldats spartiates en arrière-plan portent un bouclier basé sur celui des figurines contemporaines de guerriers en plomb, retrouvées dans le reliquaire d'Artémis Orthia.

G: L'armée spartiate, vers 470 av. J.-C. Cette planche représente une scène derrière la ligne de bataille de l'armée de Lakédémonie pendant la période difficile de 475 à 450 environ, lorsque cet état du se battre pour résister à une grande révolte des ilotes messéniens et aux alliances de ses ennemis. La Figure G1 sacrifie une chèvre à Artémis Agrotera avant l'avancée finale vers les lignes ennemies. Derrière lui, un joueur de pipeau et un trompette (G2, G3).

H: La première bataille de Mantinée, 418 av. J.-C. Sur cette planche, nous voyons les soldats au repos après la première bataille de Mantinée. La figure H1 représente un hoplite lakédémonien de la période. Derrière lui, la figure H2 représente un jeune officier, son casque-pilos décoré d'un panache. La figure H3 représente un commandant lakédémonien. Sur le sol, gise l'un des Mantinéens.

I: La flotte de Lysandre à Aigospotamoi, 405 av. J.-C. Il semble que les rameurs utilisés par toutes les flottes pendant cette campagne aient été embauchés, comme le timonnier (I 1) et les autres marins qualifiés de l'équipage. En plus de son équipage, chaque bateau avait un complément de soldats. La figure I 2 représente un soldat hoplite allié. La figure I 3 représente un archer naval. On imagine qu'ils ne portaient pas d'armure au cas où ils seraient forcés de nager.

J: "L'atelier de la guerre", Ephèse 396/5 av. J.-C. La figure J1 représente un officier supérieur lakédémonien. Cet officier porte tous les accoutrements qui distinguaient un lakédémonien à l'étranger. La figure J2 tente de reconstituer l'un des régiments ioniens de cavalerie mercenaire d'Agesilaos. Ce soldat de cavalerie ionien est basé sur les héros lakédémoniens Castor et Polydeukes, tels qu'ils sont représentés sur ces vases. La Figure J3 représente un peintre éphésien, qui porte un mélange de vêtements grecs et perses, chose sans doute courante dans la ville.

K: Régiments d'infanterie mercenaires, 396/5 av. J.-C. La figure K1 représente un mercenaire Kyreioi qui accompagna Cyrus le Jeune dans sa campagne de 401. La figure K2 est un mercenaire "Derkylidéen" au service du général Derkylideias pendant la campagne de Troade en 399. La figure K3 est un archer lourdement armuré, équipé d'une cuirasse composée.

L: Une échauffourée près de Tanagra, 377 av. J.-C. Un soldat de cavalerie lakédémonien de la fin du Ve / début du IVe siècle (L1) ressemblait sans doute aux héros nationaux à cheval, Castor et Polydeukes, qui sont souvent représentés sur les bas-reliefs de cette date. Le Skiritan (L2) est basé sur un bas-relief attique, qui représente peut-être un soldat de ce type. L'hoplite de Thèbes (L3) porte une version ancienne du casque béotien, qui fut sans doute adopté par l'infanterie au IVe siècle.

DIE FARBTAFELN

A: Krieger zur Zeit von Lykurg Diese Farbtafel zeigt das Erscheinungsbild von drei Kriegern Spartas während der letzten Jahrzehnte des 8. Jahrhunderts, als Helos versklavt war und der Machtbereich der Spartaner bis zur Eurotas-Mündung reichte. Zu dieser Zeit war der Hopliten-Schild noch nicht entwickelt und die Hopliten-Taktik noch nicht eingeführt worden. Die drei abgebildeten Figuren weisen sehr frühe „Prototypen" der traditionellen Hopliten-Beinschienen auf, die kaum das ganze Schienbein bedeckten und noch nicht die Muskulatur darstellen sollten.

B: Der Zweite Messenische Krieg Diese Farbtafel ist einer Schlachtszene auf einer spätprotokorinthischen Ära nachempfunden, die sich einst in der Chigi-Sammlung befand, nachempfunden und zeigt einen Pfeifer. Mancherorts ist man der Ansicht, daß der Einsatz von Pfeifern einst allgemein üblich war. Man weiß allerdings nur vom Heer Spartas mit Gewißheit, daß es Pfeifer einsetzte. Daher ist es möglich, daß der Künstler den Pfeifer absichtlich darstellte, um zu zeigen, daß es sich bei der Abbildung um das Heer Spartas handelte. Es könnte sich um eine der frühesten farbigen Darstellungen der Hopliten Spartas handeln.

C: Die Könige Spartas, frühes 6. Jahrhundert Eine Terrakotta-Plakette aus Sparta zeigt zwei Krieger, deren Helme mit einer quersitzenden Helmzier versehen sind. In der späteren griechischen Militärpraxis kann der Rang durch die Art der Helmzier erkenntlich gemacht werden, daher ist es möglich, daß es sich bei diesen beiden Kriegern um die beiden Könige von Sparta handelte. Die Farben auf der Innen- und Außenseite der Schilde der beiden Könige (C1, C2) beruhen auf einer Miniatur-Terrakotta-Plakette aus Sparta. C3 ist einer Statuette eines Kriegers Lakoniens nachempfunden, die in Olympia gefunden wurde. Die Abbildung wurde auf dieser Farbtafel miteinbezogen, da der ungewöhnliche Helm, der aus einer Reihe von Platten besteht, von Interesse ist.

D: Krieger aus Sparta, ca. 530 v.Chr. Die Figur D1 basiert auf der Kriegerstatuette aus Longa. Die Figur D2, deren Abbildung auf einer Statuette eines Kriegers aus Lakonien aus Dodona beruht, trägt einen Helm des illyrischen Typs, der so genannt wird, weil viele der frühen Funde aus Illyrien stammen. Nicht alle Hopliten bedienten sich dann der neuen schützenden Rüstung, wie die Figur D3 zeigt, die einer Statuette eines Kriegers aus Lakonien, die heute im Athener Nationalmuseum steht, nachempfunden ist.

E: Die Schlacht bei Thermopylen 480 v. Chr. Betrachtet man die Persischen Kriege als die glorreichste Zeit in der Geschichte Spartas, so war die Schlacht bei Thermopylen gewiß Spartas Sternstunde. Im Anfangsstadium der letzten Schlacht fügten die Griechen den Persern schwere Verluste zu und töteten zwei Brüder von Xerxes. Auch Leonidas fiel der Schlacht zum Opfer. Nach einem verzweifelten Kampf wurde seine Leiche geborgen werden, und die Griechen zogen sich auf einen kleinen Hügel am Zugang des Passes zurück, um noch einmal tapfer Widerstand zu leisten. In dieser Phase der Schlacht hatten viele Griechen bereits erlebt, daß man ihnen die Speere in den Händen entzwei brach. Andere hatten ihr Schwert verloren und mußten mit ihren bloßen Händen und Zähnen weiterkämpfen. Die Perser beschlossen, sie nur mit Wurfgeschossen zu vernichten, um weitere Verluste in den eigenen Reihen zu vermeiden.

F: Amompharetos bei der Schlacht bei Platää, 479 v.Chr. Auf der rechten Seite steht der athenische Herold (F1). Die Herolde waren durch das Zepter, das sie trugen, erkenntlich. Auf der linken Seite sieht man Darstellungen von Pausanias (F2) und Euryanax (F3) hinter ihm, die auf der Wadsworth Athenaeum-Statuette beruhen. In der Mitte ist Amompharetos (F4), dessen Abbildung der Statuette aus Dodona nachempfunden ist. Die Soldaten Spartas, die im Hintergrund dem Geschehen zusehen, haben Schilder mit Verzierungen, die auf Abbildungen auf Bleifiguren von Kriegern aus dem Schrein von Artemis Orthia beruhen.

G: Das Heer Spartas, ca. 470 v.Chr. Diese Farbtafel zeigt eine Szene hinter der Kampflinie des lakedaimonischen Heers in der schwierigen Zeit um 475-450, als der Staat gegen einen großen Aufstand der messenischen Heloten und verbündete Feinde um seinen Fortbestand kämpfen mußte. Die Figur G1 opfert vor dem letzten Vorstoß auf die feindlichen Linien Artemis Agrotera eine Ziege. Dahinter stehen ein Pfeifer und ein Trompeter (G2, G3).

H: Die erste Schlacht bei Mantineia, 418 v. Chr. Auf dieser Farbtafel sieht man Soldaten, die sich nach der ersten Schlacht bei Mantineia ausruhen. Bei der Figur H1 handelt es sich um einen lakedaimonischen Hopliten der Zeit. Die Figur H2 dahinter ist ein rangniedriger Offizier, dessen Pilos-Helm mit einem Federbusch geschmückt ist. Die Figur H3 stellt einen lakedaimonischen Oberbefehlshaber dar. Auf dem Boden liegt einer der Gefallenen von Mantineia.

I: Lysanders Flotte bei Aigospotamoi, 405 v.Chr. Anscheinend waren die Ruderer aller Flotten während dieses Feldzugs angeheuert. Das Gleiche gilt auch für die Steuermänner (I1) und die anderen leitenden, ausgebildeten Matrosen der Mannschaft. Außer der Besatzung verfügte jedes Schiff über zusätzliche Marinetruppen. Bei der Figur I2 handelt es sich um einen Marinesoldaten verbündeter Hopliten. Die Figur I3 stellt einen Marine-Bogenschützen dar. Es ist anzunehmen, daß diese Soldaten keine Rüstung trugen, falls sie gezwungen sein sollten zu schwimmen.

J: Die „Kriegswerkstatt", Ephesus, 396/5 v.Chr. Bei der Figur J1 handelt es sich um den ranghöchsten Offizier Lakedaimons. Er trägt alle Kleidungsstücke, die einen Lakedaimonier im Ausland erkenntlich machten. Die Figur J2 versucht eine Rekonstruktion eines der ionischen Söldnerkavallerie-Regimenter von Agesilaos. Diese Abbildung eines ionischen Kavalleristen beruht auf den lakedaimonischen Helden Kastor und Polydeukes, die man auf diesen Vasen sieht. Die Figur J3 stellt einen Maler aus Ephesus dar, der mit einer Mischung aus griechischen und persischen Kleidungsstücken bekleidet ist, was in der Stadt unter Umständen üblich war.

K: Söldner-Infanterieregimenter, 396/5 v.Chr. Bei der Figur K1 handelt es sich um einen kyrenischen Söldner, der Kyros d.J. 401 auf seinem Feldzug begleitete. Die Figur K2 ist ein „derkylideianischer" Söldner im Dienste des Generals Derkylideias während des Troas-Feldzugs 399. Bei der Figur K3 handelt es sich um einen Bogenschützen in schwerer Rüstung mit einem zusammengesetzten Küraß.

L: Ein Gefecht in der Nähe von Tanagra, 377 v.Chr. Ein lakedaimonischer Kavallerist ähnelte im späten 5. und 4. Jahrhundert (L1) wahrscheinlich den berittenen Nationalhelden Kastor und Polydeukes, die häufig auf Reliefs aus dieser Zeit abgebildet sind. Der Skiritanier (L2) basiert auf einem attischen Relief und zeigt möglicherweise einen Soldaten dieser Art. Der Hoplit aus Theben (L3) trägt eine frühe Version des böotischen Helms, den die Infanterie im 4. Jahrhundert wahrscheinlich übernahm.